A COUNTRYMAN'S YEAR

A COUNTRYMAN'S YEAR

Thurlow Craig

With drawings by Bill Martin

Introduced by
Peter Haining

SOUVENIR PRESS

First published 1988 by Souvenir Press Ltd,
43 Great Russell Street, London WC1B 3PA
and simultaneously in Canada
Reprinted 1990

ISBN 0 285 63000 8

Printed in Great Britain by
The Guernsey Press Co. Ltd, Guernsey, Channel Islands.

CONTENTS

THURLOW CRAIG
*Everyman
of the
Countryside*

For millions of people Thurlow Craig was as much a part of
Sunday mornings as bacon and eggs, a walk in the park or a
drink in the local pub at lunchtime. He was a tonic more
eagerly sought than the international news or the gossip of
high society, even the sports results. Week in and week out
he brought the essence of the countryside, its wildlife and
ever-changing seasons, into the homes of readers, whether
they lived in the heart of a big city or in the same kind of
idyllic rural setting that he himself had chosen.

With a perceptive eye and a keen appreciation of the
world about him—married to an easy and engrossing
literary style—Thurlow Craig observed and chronicled
nature at first hand in all its varieties. He was described by
the *Sunday Express*, the newspaper to which he contributed
for almost thirty years, as its 'Nature Correspondent'.
But to those who held his work in the highest esteem—
and they were many—he was much more: an Everyman of
the Countryside, a Boswell of the Wilds.

Although during a lifetime spent in many of the remote
corners of the earth he produced a variety of books and
articles, it was for his weekly column, 'Up Country', in the
Sunday Express that he was best known and will be longest
remembered. For it was in these essays that he wrote
so movingly of the wildlife which abounded close to the
doors of his little stone-built, two-bedroomed house at
Pantfynnonlas near Lampeter in the remote Cambrian
Hills of Dyfed.

His companions here were not the exotic animals of
South America he had once trailed on horseback, but the
more modest yet infinitely fascinating squirrels, hedge-

hogs, voles, owls, badgers, mice, toads and birds of the nearby hills and woods; not to mention the sheep, cattle and livestock of neighbouring farms. In the sanctuary of his home were to be found cats like Prudy, the white tom, Black Tom the polydactyl, and Tabitha the stray he welcomed as his own. He wrote of his dogs, too—Teena the hunt terrier, and Holly the Rottweiler bitch. In the yard outside were to be found geese, bantams, donkeys, goats and a skewbald pony, Patchy, perhaps the one reminder of the roaming life he had once led. All these animals—and their predecessors —became as familiar to his readers over the years as their own pets—together with all the other forms of wildlife that flocked to his little farm and crowded through his days and into his prose.

The little house where Thurlow Craig lived—its Welsh name meaning "the Blue Well in the Dingle"—was as rugged as the man himself: isolated yet resilient, boasting no running water (this had to be fetched from a well 75 yards down the hill), its stout walls honeycombed with mouse-holes that provided a haven for mice, squirrels, bats and beetles; yet still it was infused with his love of nature and for his second wife, Ann, who shared his life-long passion for the wilds.

Charles William Thurlow Craig was born in 1902 and early showed evidence of the thirst for adventure which was to drive him throughout his life when, at the tender age of 13, he lied about his birth date in order to be able to serve with the Royal Navy during the First World War. Following three years at sea, he headed for the wilds of South America where he gathered some of the raw materials which were to enliven his later books. His natural skill as a rider found him employment as, in turn, a horseman, cowboy and gaucho.

Returning to England just before the outbreak of the Second World War, he was able to put his facility for living in the wilds, along with his courage and resourcefulness, to good use by working in the Resistance Movement in Europe. His companion in many of the dangerous operations he undertook was his first wife, Mitzi, who died in 1968.

Thurlow Craig had also discovered his talent as a writer

and the titles of his books—now out of print and, sadly, hard to find—read almost like an autobiography. *A Rebel for a Horse* and *Paraguayan Interlude* describe his South American adventures; *White Girls Eastward* and *Plague over London* show his fine reporting powers at work; while *The Swamp of Cardelli* and *West of Rio Grande* are superb travelogues. *Spinner's Delight* features another of his great interests, fishing, and is a mine of information for the expert and layman alike.

But it was in his column, 'Up Country', which he began to write for the *Sunday Express* from 2 June 1957, that he found the most rewarding expression for his love of the countryside. Here he wrote of his new life as a Welsh hill-farmer with warmth, sensitivity and without an ounce of resentment towards anything, creature or element, that crossed his path. His was the authentic voice of the countryside, and small wonder his words struck an immediate chord in the hearts of his readers. Their admiration for him became unbounded over the years, and at his funeral in Lampeter in 1985, the presiding Methodist minister, Mr Morgan Llewellyn-Jones, observed, "The affection with which the readers of the *Sunday Express* held him was shown by the fact that if ever his column was missing from the paper, the Editor was inundated with letters from people demanding to know when it would return."

It is for these readers—and indeed for all those who enjoy nature writing at its best—that this selection of essays from the 'Up Country' series has been assembled as a memorial to his unique contribution to our understanding of all God's creatures. It is also a celebration of the man himself, for his unique personality shines through his prose, as does the very obvious fact that he was a *character* in the true sense of the word! He was one of a dying breed in our commercialised and ever more technological world.

In the pages of this book the reader can share Thurlow Craig's affection and respect for all animals, and his love of the countryside. Despite his awareness of what was happening in towns and cities, he still managed to find beauty in the world, and by his words he enabled his readers to see through his eyes. As one reader, also a Welshman, wrote to the *Sunday Express* immediately after the columnist's death, "Thank you for the enjoyment Thurlow Craig has given me over the last 30 years. His articles were always real as he portrayed nature as both beautiful and cruel, very often at the same time. I suspect that Thurlow Craig might, when the Gates of Heaven are opened, stop a while to watch a spider spinning its web on the hinge."

When Thurlow Craig died of a stroke at the age of 83 on Tuesday, 15 September, 1985, the *Sunday Express* lost a valued contributor, but its readers lost a very real *friend*. No more would his weekly despatches from the remote small-holding in Wales be an inseparable part of Sunday mornings. His writings, however, remain as his testament, and so long as they survive, the world he described will never be allowed to pass away.

Peter Haining
Boxford, Suffolk.
May 1988.

January

New Year's Day was exceptional; dry, frosty and calm. So out we stepped after a disgracefully full breakfast for a long mountain walk with the dogs.

Holly the Rottweiler is always as good as gold on a walk in the open-range hills but her friend Teena, the little Jack Russell bitch, who at one time in her life had obviously been a hunt terrier, is not so well behaved. She goes nearly mad if she sees or hears hounds about and I have always kept her on the lead in the hills; until New Year's Day, that is.

For there were no loose sheep anywhere to be seen as they had all been taken away to winter in a lower altitude nearer their home farms. So she was allowed to run free.

We got Teena three years ago from a dog rescue home and the first time we took her out we unthinkingly let her off the chain as soon as we got to open, unfenced land, and away she ran after a young rabbit, across the valley, over another hill, and out of sight.

We had quite a chase before finding her. No damage was done, but that was the last time she was allowed to run free in the hills.

This time there was no trouble. At first she wouldn't go more than about 20 yards away from us. But we encouraged her to get along and join Holly, who usually ranges to and fro between 70 and 80 yards ahead. Every time she got over that distance she was whistled to heel and came racing back, with little Teena following her example, going flat out and sometimes getting back first.

Finally there came a real test. We all walked over the brow of a steep hill overlooking a deepish valley, and on the other side but heading towards us on the same path we were using was a small bunch of sheep nicely grouped with their owner and two dogs herding them along. These had obviously strayed from the lowland flock and were now being brought back.

My wife whistled as usual, and the first to turn was Teena, who shot back to us well ahead of Holly, both dogs taking station beautifully at heel.

We all turned aside to make way for the approaching little flock and they all went past, not taking any notice of the dogs, nor the dogs of them. As their owner drew level with us he turned aside to have a word with us—and the word was very kind, all about how well kept and well trained our dogs were, that the local sheep on our neighbouring mountains knew all about them and never take the slightest notice of them.

Then on we went home, well pleased that the year had started on such a happy note.

* * *

Hedgehogs are rum beasts in more ways than one. They are ordinarily beasts of the night, avoiding daylight whenever possible, save for one exception; if there is a heavy daytime thunderstorm accompanied by heavy summer heat, they will emerge in full sunlight to feast upon the wealth of slugs and snails that are lured out of their daytime sluggishness.

So also in winter. Unlike squirrels and dormice they do not lay up a winter store of food, and on a fine winter's day will interrupt their winter sleep to get what food they can.

So far, our own hedge-pigs show no signs of making a permanent hibernation, as I was reminded the other night.

Shortly after the sun had vanished below the high hills behind us, I sneaked down to my usual hidey-hole by the skull paddock to see if perchance a fox or badger might be about.

It was still quite warm and I settled down comfortably to wait. And I did not have to wait long. Earlier that day a buzzard, seeing masses of variegated tits covering a large lump of suet hanging from a blackthorn tree had sent the little birds flying and prepared to attack that suet.

Fortunately he had been seen by three of our resident ravens who immediately came up in line abreast—battle formation. And attack they did. In about five seconds the buzzard was in full flight homewards, and the suet was on the ground.

I resolved to put it back again but forgot all about it. When I was passing the spot on my way to my hidey-hole I saw it and made another resolution to attend to it before my return to the house.

I could still see it from where I sat a yard or two away and when I next looked in that direction a very fat hedgehog was feeding on it. Now, the tits had converted this lump by eating out the middle and giving it a waist so that it looked like a very fat hour-glass. And the hedgehog was also going for this part, probably because it was softer than the rest.

Presently the hedgehog was joined by a smaller one who sneaked in from the side and started to eat. The fat one made no objections and soon that lump became two—one large, one small—and at the same time I sneezed.

They did not take off, as they are used to seeing me around, but maybe thinking that I might try to take their lucky find away, the big one took up the larger section in his mouth and walked away down the hill to their exit. The small one did likewise with the smaller lump. And in a few seconds they were out of sight.

* * *

After several days of almost continuous rain the weather turned really nasty on us, finishing up with a 48-hour non-stop downpour which brought the river out in places and over the roads.

Some days ago Patchy—being a big horse he doesn't mind going through mud which is far too deep for the donkeys—was grazing on top of a bank along our east boundary-fence, which is boggy both sides.

But the donkeys did even better than that after a close inspection of the eastern boundary. They found a place where they could not only get through the fence but about ten yards away on the far side was a small patch of lush and luscious grass that hadn't been touched.

When we found them they had eaten at least half the grass but in the meantime heavy rain had made the place they had got through all boggy. And they refused to come back. They would have been belly-deep in mud.

There was only one thing to do. We dug away most of the mud and put their day's ration of hay and corn well in view on our side. I then picked up the bucket of corn and walked towards them, making much of the fact that I was only halfway up to knee-high in the mire.

I went very slowly, calling to them in dulcet tones and rattling the corn-bucket until my wife yelled at me to stop the dulcet stuff and the corn-rattling, concentrating on my feet, *in no mud at all*. This I continued to do, silent—and, by the Lord Harry, it worked.

These donkeys, the most intelligent of animals, seeing there was a safe path, broke into an instant gallop, pulling my wife face-down in the mud on their side, up the bank like lightning and down on our side. I just had time to turn and flee before they were on me, both small noses up to the eyes in that bucket. And that was that.

We were glad, because if they had refused, there would have been no way to get a tractor down there on either side of the bog. Bar getting a helicopter to lift them out it would have been entirely a man-power job and might have taken hours. However, that whole fence has now been made donkey-proof and it won't happen again.

*   *   *

Something has gone wrong with the weather. For confirmation of this turn not to the human weather-forecasters but to those with an instinctive and far more accurate knowledge of the subject—the wild birds and beasts.

One such sign among the birds is a sudden, urgent hunger for food such as that which gripped the feathered population here this week.

It was a robin which drew it to my attention.

I was lying, half awake, in bed in the dark of the morning

when there was a tapping at the bedroom window. Switching on the night-torch (a powerful 12-volt affair with a chargeable battery) I glanced at the clock. It was half an hour before daylight. I turned the light on to the window. And there was the robin, banging with his beak at the window.

Now, anyone who knows anything about birds in winter also knows that robins are intensely territorial, resenting very violently any invasion by other robins, which in normal times are soon driven away.

At this winter's start we had two. They had been here for years without any kind of invasion. A fortnight later we had four—and the strange thing was that the long-term residents didn't drive them off.

A week later our marsh-tits were there on the nearest blackthorn—at least a week before we generally begin to put out food for them. Now there are ten of them, not to mention a brace of long-tailed tits we have never had before.

But back to this dark-o'-the morning robin. After his urgent summons I got dressed then went downstairs and filled a two-pound bowl of food to the brim. Going out into the forecourt lit by the outside light, I scattered it about and went back into the house to watch from a window. The small ones I couldn't count as they crowded around to peck ravenously at the flaked maize, breaking it up before swallowing the pieces.

These small birds weigh less than on ounce apiece. Not only are they tiny; they have quite a high body temperature. So they need a constant supply of high-calorie food. And they know that the cornflakes children so eagerly consume before running off to school in the morning provide the precious quick heat that keeps the life in them.

The bigger birds, comprising our six ravens (there were only two when first they came to our breakfast-table) about a dozen carrion crows and as many jackdaws, not to mention more than that amount of magpies, were all going for the smaller stuff—oats, barley and wheat—which takes longer to digest.

The strange thing about all these birds was this: although

they were of all sizes, from a visiting red kite weighing eight or nine pounds down to a marsh-tit possibly of about half an ounce, they were all feeding peaceably. And that included the robins.

Normally feeding so many birds of different types together would be accompanied by numerous pecking-order squabbles.

So much for the uncharacteristic behaviour of the birds. Read into it what you will. For my part, I know they are frightened about the weather to come. And so, therefore, am I.

*   *   *

My fears are being realised with a vengeance.

There were a few spring-like days last week and during that time our normally overcrowded bird-feeding area was virtually deserted.

Then there was a huge drop in temperature during the night and when I was up and about in the half-light of a dark and windless morn it was minus one Centigrade.

Obviously the birds knew what was in store for them. I have never seen them packed so thickly on the forecourt.

And they were ravenous. I scattered the food from their morning bowl—a good two and a half pounds of mixed corn—and they were at it immediately. There were hundreds of them and in less than an hour that food, which on a normal winter's day would keep the birds going for between two and three hours, was all gone.

I put out another ration, then another, and altogether that day they got through about 12 pounds.

As I write there is a biting wind from the north-north-east, which is the nastiest quarter of all, and the temperature outside when I put out the first lot of corn was minus five Centigrade (23F for those who stick to the old scale).

While I was standing at the window watching the birds feed I realised that something was wrong: one of the four robins was missing.

I soon found the bird. It was on the broad top of the stone wall, its wings spread but its eyes still open.

So, ignoring the old wives' warning that it is bad luck to take a robin into the house, I brought it in to warm it up.

Presently the little creature was in a small box in the open oven while my wife warmed half an eggcup of flaked maize with a spoonful of milk. And an hour later it was sitting on the edge of the box pecking into the food and loving it. We will probably put it outside in the morning but the chances are that, having tasted the good life indoors, we shall have it pecking on the window for the rest of the winter.

*   *   *

We didn't wait until market day to do the shopping last week, just in case we became snowed in without sufficient supplies.

And we are glad we didn't delay. For there is now six inches of snow on our forecourt, which means plenty enough on the little mountain roads to stop us getting to town in the car.

However, as it was we got back without any trouble, packed with such items as paraffin for pressure lamps, propane gas for the cooker, and corn for the horse.

There was also the small matter of water both for the stock and ourselves as supplies at the house had frozen solid. The stream is still running but we can't use that because it is being contaminated by neighbouring sheep and cattle, something that can never be ruled out on these isolated mountain holdings.

We had brought water from town in a couple of big milk churns. But when the geese came up for their share our baby goose was nowhere to be seen. Presently my wife heard a noise down by the well in the west paddock, went down there and yelled to me. So I went also.

And there, lo and behold, was our youngest goose in quite a mess.

Usually the well is covered by a wooden lid to keep frogs out, but we had removed this when the goose-pond froze over with at least four inches of ice so that the geese could use what was left in the well before that, too, froze up.

Well, poor little Bertha had got down into the well for a

wash but hadn't reckoned on six or seven degrees of frost, and was now enclosed almost all over in a crisp mush of ice from which she'd never be able to extricate herself.

We got some of it off, enough for her to waddle most uncomfortably behind us up to the house, complaining at the top of her voice with every step until we got there.

Once in the living-room we shut the door to keep her relations out, putting Bertha in the old tin bath that we still have standing by for such purposes and cleaned her up in it, using expensive soap and a softish brush, until she was perfectly beautiful.

Indeed, when she got back to the others, far from being ashamed of herself for getting into such a predicament, she strutted to and fro as proud as any peacock, so pleased was she to have become the family's most glamorous member.

*   *   *

My wife had gone out with Holly, the Rottweiler bitch, and our little ex-hunt terrier, Teena, leaving me in a semi-comatose state in my rocker in front of a bright fire.

Just when I thought I was in for a spell of perfect peace on a cold January day, back they came, all in a state of extreme excitement.

Apparently they had run all the way home after finding a week-old calf with its neck stuck through a fence.

The youngster, it seemed, would not last long as its frantic mother, a Welsh Black, was knocking it about all over the place, trying to extricate it. These hardy Welsh cattle spend all year outdoors, unlike their lowland cousins.

A wire cutter was needed, and that meant I had to accompany the rescue party as my wife's wire cutter had gone missing a few days previously, and she is unable to use mine, which is rather primitive.

Having found mine, we set off at a brisker pace than I like, but which brought us to the trapped calf, quickly . . . if in a state of puffedness. We waved off the cow and assessed the situation. At first sight it looked dire.

When found by my wife the animal had only its head through the wire, but now, not more than ten minutes later, both front feet and one hind leg were well and truly stuck, mainly due to the cow's good, though misguided, intentions.

It was a question now of Teena and Holly (with my wife's help) keeping the cow at bay while I freed the calf with my almost Stone Age cutter.

This did not take long, but was done at the expense of the fence.

It would take the owner the rest of the afternoon to repair it, but no matter: we had saved him a valuable calf, and we rang him up to inform him when we returned home.

* * *

Thanks to the snow, we know that a hare comes every night or early morning to get a share of what is going around the house.

The other day we decided to follow the footprints to find out where it is lying up. And just as I thought, the prints gradually converged until, about 60 yards from the north boundary fence, they became a solid three-inch wide track. Just short of the fence itself, built on top of the low remains of a dry-stone wall, the track suddenly ended, but continued for a short distance on the other side.

Now the fence is about five feet high and of course any hare can negotiate such a jump with perfect ease. But the take-off and landing points at the favoured crossing point are a dead giveaway. And this is what we had come to investigate, and why we had brought a rake.

For there are foxes about, to say nothing of the wild polecat, a very formidable beast and no less a killer on land than his cousin, the mink-gone-wild. And the polecat loves hares just as much as the mink loves salmon.

On the other side of the fence we quietly walked up to a snowdrift where all tracks ended and there, under the remains of a discarded fence post, surrounded by and almost covered with snow, was the hare. Only the hare's eyes and nose showed, and doubtless she hoped we had not seen her.

Silently we withdrew, and when a few yards away

started to rake lightly over the tracks. When about 80 yards from the hare we scattered drops of Jeyes Fluid, which has a smell that foxes and polecats equate with human beings and avoid, whereas the hare would already be well acquainted with the smell, because whenever stables, goat-pens, chicken runs and the forecourt are mucked off, Jeyes is always used.

And that was that. Until next snowfall (and who knows when that will be?) our hare is as safe as can be from hungry predators.

*   *   *

The thaw started after we had had eight or nine days of very cold days and nights, the daytime temperature never above minus three degrees Centigrade, dropping at dusk to minus four or five, with early morning temperatures—except one—between seven and ten below zero.

That one exception was the night before the thaw began. When I got up at six in the morning it was down to minus 13—our record low. Now we seem to be in a fairly warm and extremely wet period.

In such weather you do not expect much song from any of the bird-table population but this is the time of year when some small birds start trying their voices out; getting into tune, you might say, so that come the real springtime they will be in full voice.

Birds that start this early (provided that there is not a foot of snow on the ground with sub-zero temperatures day and night), are first the robin. He perches himself on a fairly low bare bough and pipes up mournfully, not much in tune.

Next is the hedge-sparrow, who is not a sparrow at all, although very similar in plumage. The correct name is accentor. His voice is at present very feeble, although he is a cheerful little thing.

Blackbirds and song-thrushes also have a try in a warm January spell, though this is also very far from the real thing.

There is one outstanding exception: the missel-thrush. And by the way, some nature books spell it "mistle", which is wrong. This comes from the belief that this thrush eats mistletoe berries, which it does not. Indeed, as far as I know there is no bird or small animal which eats mistletoe.

The word "missel" comes from the Anglo-Saxon word meaning "big", which is very apt. The song-thrush is between eight and nine inches long. The fieldfare, a winter visitor, is ten inches long (as is the blackbird). But the missel-thrush at 11 in. long, beats them all.

Another name for him is storm-cock, because he sings at his best in a gale-force wind with torrential rain. I have a delightful picture of him in one of my old nature books. There he perches on a bare bough dressed in sou'wester and oilskins, facing the storm and singing away as though fit to burst.

We had such a day before the present warm spell. There on the forecourt in front of the living-room window was a great mass of birds. The wind was blowing at gale force from the north-east, the rain was turning to sleet and the temperature was minus four degrees C.

The storm-cock appeared from nowhere, alighted on the forecourt and immediately noticed the cows' cornflakes amongst the other types of birdfood. These he attacked gladly for a couple of minutes, then flew up on to the topmost branch of the nearest blackthorn.

Facing the wind, he was in full song, perfectly tuned, for about a minute. We opened the window and heard him clearly—although it has to be said that he is not as melodious as the song-thrush or blackbird.

Then down he flew to feed for a couple of minutes more, then returned to his tree and sang again. Once more he fed, sang for his breakfast, and was then away.

Twice since then we have seen him feeding here, and I hope he stays all winter.

*   *   *

We did not expect the speed and ferocity of the latest cold spell which caught us, here, completely unready. Fortunately, though, it gave us enough warning to get to town for supplies in the middle of the first flurry of snow.

But by the time we got back the snow and ice had made our very short downhill drive from the top road to our main entry gate more like a skating-rink all over, and a very dangerous one, too.

Unable to stop, we slid down in the car quite happily, ending up halfway along the forecourt, fortunately without causing any damage. At least we were that much nearer to unloading the several hundredweight of corn of various kinds that we had brought for the stock and our countless number of wild birds.

Within an hour of returning we had four coconuts split and hanging up in a blackthorn, with a couple of peanut nets for the tits, although many other birds were also making acrobatic use of them.

They included half-a-dozen marauding magpies which in our estimation are the worst-mannered birds of all. But one can't help feeling sorry for them in this sort of weather.

Holly, our Rottweiler, from inside the living-room, on her chair in front of the window, did her best to scare them off, but made so much noise banging on the window and emitting her eldritch bellows, that I couldn't concentrate on my newspaper.

However, pretty soon one jump up from the chair and one angry bark was enough for those birds and they would depart for the lower paddock where a couple of fresh oxheads had been newly put out for them. And I could read my precious paper—after a fashion.

Actually that paddock, specially stocked for the predators, already had numerous ravens, carrion crows, buzzards and magpies, plus one solitary jay and upwards of 20 smaller birds that did not fear the predators, all bunched over the fresher oxheads and other bits and pieces that had been put down for them.

The birds are virtually the only type of wildlife to be seen on this hill at the moment, and our bird-table has been valuable not only from the food point of view, but in enabling us to spot a feathered creature needing special help, generally due to the weather, but occasionally due to one of our cats.

And I'm more than glad to say that we certainly have

two, and possibly all three, of our little wrens still alive, and that is something with temperatures down to minus 10 Centigrade.

*   *   *

After several heavy snowfalls our narrow mountain roads were impassable for some days. But being cut off is no great hardship in the short term—all the farms around here are well stocked with food for man and beast.

We have very little stock and they are all shut in every night, which is not to say that they don't spend all day inside too, in bad weather.

Satisfying the appetites of the wild birds is at least as big a problem. I won't tell you the total cost because you wouldn't believe it. But nearly six kilos of peanuts alone are accounted for each week by the tits, a few acrobatic chaffinches, and two or three nut-hatches.

We put the nuts in those hanging wire nets, placing them so that we have a good view from the living-room window.

The other day when my wife went to feed the bantams at daybreak something appeared between her feet, and by the pressure lamp light she saw two gleaming eyes looking up at her. It was our hedgehog, which we usually see perhaps once a month, except in the winter.

Then, when my wife made her way back to the house the hedge-pig followed, before waiting patiently at the left side of the doorstep where her regular saucers of bread and milk were placed last year.

Telling her to stay there, my wife soon had a small soup plate containing warm milk, scraps of bread and small bits of meat and veg.—not the most appetising of breakfasts. But that beast took not the slightest notice of us, though we were within two feet of her, until she had finished.

Then she looked up at us with little twinkling eyes, and my wife swears she said something . . . and who am I to say her nay?

After that the little creature turned and made her way, not across the forecourt and down the house paddock, the way she usually goes to her lair, but back to the bantam's loosebox, vanishing through that door.

Obviously she had decided to stay with us, building a nest in a draughtless corner under a rainproof manger where she can sleep the winter out unmolested by man or beast, just coming forth if a horse stamping his noisy feet in the adjoining loosebox wakes her up and she feels like a spot of breakfast.

Later we noticed an untidy pile of hay in a corner of the bantams' box. No matter how cold it gets she will be all right there, until spring comes.

February

Moles are anathema to the gardener, the horticulturalist and groundsmen wherever ball games are played on grass.

Yet I remember old Harry, our mole catcher, making quite a comfortable living out of them. Outside his cottage were masses of old doors and other bits of discarded wood all facing the sun, where the little pelts were stretched out.

When they were thoroughly dried out he would packet them by the dozen until he had a sackful, put that over the handlebars of his bike and pedal down to the local mole and rabbit man, who paid out a few old pence per pelt.

It has often occurred to me that moles have much in common with shrews. Both have voracious appetites and must feed every few hours otherwise they die. Both need short and numerous sleeping periods (they start searching for food immediately they wake up). And both are decidedly hot tempered.

Because fresh casts do not appear in very cold weather many people believe that moles hibernate. But they do not. The reason for the lack of molehills during prolonged hard frosts is that the worms, leatherjackets and wireworms are much deeper down. So the hungry mole has to follow.

On our smallholding this winter it has been very noticeable that new mole casts are thrown up immediately the snow melts after a cold spell.

From our kitchen windows we have a good view of the west paddock where, as soon as the last cold snap thawed, new molehills popped up all over the place.

A few days ago, while I was making the morning tea, I saw a new one heave up not three yards from the kitchen. Out came a mole which ran towards the house, straight for the dish of water that we put out for the bantams. Putting his spade-like forepaws over the edge, he hoisted himself up and began to drink.

I already knew that moles are also voracious drinkers. But I was surprised to see how much that little creature took.

Then I was given a perfect illustration of how bad tempered the furry little beasts are.

Up came another mole. Like the first he put his "spades" on the rim of the dish, got his little head over the top, and saw the other across the bowl. In fact, they both saw each other at the same moment. And down they got to the chase, though unfortunately, as they were both running round the bowl anti-clockwise, there was at first no chance of a head-on collision.

Then one turned, and the battle was on. I have no idea which won, but one scampered off and disappeared into the nearest molehill. The other had a drink before scuttling down the molehill too.

So I suppose that while I made my tea, these moles were still battling it out in the dark depths.

*　　*　　*

When we bought this smallholding some years ago it was badly neglected.

There was no mains water-supply, and there still isn't at this level and I don't suppose there ever will be. For few of us live up here.

This doesn't stop the council trying to wring water rates out of us, though.

Nor was there any refuse collection—and there still isn't. We take our own garbage to the nearest refuse tip generally once a week. And this system has worked admirably until recently when my wife and I fell sick, I with winter flu which was not serious and my wife with a lung infection brought about through handling hay.

All this being so, our garbage mounted up near the back door. There are now six sacks neatly lined up against the outside wall in which there is a window with one pane missing, that the cats use.

Among these is Black Tom, a seven-toed, all-black tom given to us a few weeks ago by a friend. He was rather wild at first and had a strong objection to women. He took wonderfully well to the other cats, dogs and to me as well, but wouldn't have anything to do with my wife at all until the other night.

At about 3 a.m. my wife was woken up by alarming sounds from outside. She rushed downstairs, switching on the lights, and opened the back door.

And there it was: a half-empty garbage sack dancing about all over the floor, with fearful sounds bursting out of it. The mouth of this sack was blocked by a full one which had apparently fallen over on to it.

My wife lifted the full sack away and stood back, because she had already been badly scratched once by Black Tom, whose voice she had recognised.

Out shot the cat, still screeching and on three legs—for the other was stuck inside a small can. He banged through the cat-trap at the bottom of the kitchen door, and carried on screeching indoors. In went my wife and very bravely picked him up, pulled the can off and dropped him on the floor.

Black sat down, lifted the trapped paw, looked at it, sniffed, gave it a lick and then, of all things, made a high tail and rubbed himself against my wife's bare leg, purring loudly.

So now they are the best of friends. But now we are careful to leave an empty space beneath the window, so that the cats can come and go at will without having to cross those refuse sacks.

*   *   *

The weathermen had warned about a huge and fierce cold belt travelling slowly against westerly winds which would reduce its ferocity.

All happened as forecast except that the wind changed.

Instead of coming warm from the Atlantic it came bitterly

cold and with blizzard force from the east and that ruined everything. Vast drifts piled up everywhere and the bottom dropped out of all the thermometers from John o' Groats to Land's End.

The night before last we had a low night temperature of minus 12 Centigrade and last night it went down to minus 11.

The dogs had hardly been out for days and were madly wanting a walk. So, even though every walking surface we know of within miles is like an ice rink, out we set.

I was carrying a heavy hammer in one pocket, anticipating that when we got to our destination we should need it, and so we did.

We got to the little pond that we had an eye on but before we could stop her Holly the Rottweiler jumped happily on to the surface because from the bank it looked exactly like open water. But of course it was thick ice and poor Holly dashed with all brakes on at a good 20 miles an hour right across it and came up short with a despairing yell when her nose hit the bank.

She got to her feet looking very sheepish, to stand beside us while I got out the hammer and started to break up the ice.

Near the bank it was solid right down to the bottom but further in there was water under five or six inches of ice. From there on it was quite quick work to clear the ice away from a large patch.

The reason for this was that there were ponies in the field with no other water supply, plus a pair of mallards that had been living nearby for quite a while and seemed likely to make their nest there. But they had not allowed for deep-freeze conditions with a total lack of water.

On our way back home we looked back to the pond, now far below. Already the two mallards were swimming around in the new patch of water. And behind them were the three ponies that had evidently already had their drink.

Our little effort had been useful and with that happy thought in our hearts we turned our frozen faces towards home and hot drinks.

*　　*　　*

Once or twice during this strange blow-hot, blow-cold winter, I have noticed the scarcity of both red and grey squirrels. Here we only know of one pair of our native reds—which have been very scarce for years—and we have not seen even these for many weeks now.

The greys, imported from the States about 130 years ago, are listed as pests and until the middle 'fifties there was a bounty of half-a-crown per tail. When that was cancelled they began to multiply and until two years ago when the hazel nut crop failed (it failed again this year) the greys were numerous.

Now, though, they are more scarce than ever. In normal times we would see three or four when driving to or from our market town but the last time I saw one was at the start of this winter's first really cold spell.

I had come down early because a tomtit had got into my workroom during the previous afternoon and I had not discovered it until night-time. Knowing it would not be able to get to its winter quarters in the dense darkness with a gale blowing and sleet falling in a temperature of minus 2C, I put down a bit of fat and half a coconut for it to feed on and left it there.

Then, in the morning, as I opened the window to let it out, I saw something sitting on an oxhead I had put in the lower paddock for the predatory birds to feed on.

It was not until I got the spyglass that I could see it was a grey squirrel, and as the light grew stronger I saw that the wretched little animal was just skin and bone, eating as fast as possible because it knew that the stronger the light the more danger he was in.

Then it came; two of our resident ravens flew down to the attack, buzzing him while screaming for their last year's children to come and help. As these nest less than 40 yards from the cottage, they arrived almost immediately and the grey realised that discretion was the better part of valour.

He jumped down off the oxhead and turned to run and I was able to see that his belly was nicely extended. Then he was away down the paddock at full speed as the four ravens buzzed him furiously. Considering his condition—not to mention the weight of his meal—his speed was astonishing and before he had gone 20 yards he suddenly turned sharp left to the safety of a bramble thicket.

The ravens returned for their breakfast and I did not see the squirrel again. But he must have been there considerably before dawn to have filled himself up so well. Almost certainly he will come again by night and, if he is wise, will leave well before full daylight.

It may surprise some readers to hear that squirrels eat meat. Indeed they do. In springtime they are not above eating fledglings that fall out of their nests and I once saw a grey squirrel chasing a baby rabbit.

*   *   *

As I write the drifts are slowly melting away and will all be gone within a week if we get no more snow.

A couple of days ago I heard a blackbird trying out his vocal cords with a view, possibly, to beginning his spring song. And one could not blame him. For since the thaw started the weather has been so mild that any bird might think that spring was not only on the way but practically here already.

Many of our non-migrant birds are busy nest-making or repairing and I should not be at all surprised if some of them are already sitting.

If so I'm afraid they could be in for a big disappointment if we get another cold snap.

I've also noticed a very large hedgehog several times on the bird-table, feeding on the oxheads put down for the predatory birds and beasts. As the hedgehog mainly eats meat when he can find it, he is more than welcome.

People sometimes ask whether they should feed sluggish hedgehogs if they arrive at the door in winter when they should be asleep.

The answer is Yes. Give them warm bread and milk with a piece of any kind of meat you may have left over. But if you happen to come across a dormant hedgehog in winter or even in early spring, on no account wake it up to give it a feed because you could easily kill it.

On mild days in winter you may see one lumbering about in the garden, particularly if there is enough sun after rain with a warm enough day to bring a few snails or slugs out.

I found out years ago that although a hedgehog will instantly kill one of the big black ones, this is only killing for its own sake. He'll not eat it. For hedgehogs prefer snails and small white slugs. Apparently the black ones are either nasty-tasting or possibly even poisonous.

So if you accidentally get landed with a lively young beast in winter and he shows signs of wanting to stay, it might be kind to put him up for the rest of the winter if you have somewhere to lodge him, such as under the stairs or in a passageway that can be shut off from dogs or cats.

But do not disturb him if he shows any signs of going back to a permanent sleep until the real warm weather arrives.

* * *

I cannot believe those reports that wild puma-type cats have been sighted in various parts of Britain.

If such animals really were on the loose we would soon have more evidence than the odd fleeting glimpse. For there is no mistaking the killing method of the puma, alias cougar, alias mountain lion.

The nearest relative in Britain is the Scottish wild cat, unbelievably ferocious and said to be quite untameable. But, of course, at no more than 3 ft 9 in. from nose to tip of tail, it is nowhere near a puma's size.

I've lived in this wild part of west Wales for more than 20 years and in all that time have never seen a real wild cat although I've seen their spoors and know they are about as rare as the polecats.

On the night of the last full moon I went down to the field of skulls where we feed the predators such as foxes, badgers, ravens and crows, not to mention any polecat that cares to visit us.

It was almost as bright as day under the moon in a windless, cloudless sky. I'd been sitting on the bank under a tree and just thinking about going inside because there

were about five degrees of frost freezing my ears and nose,
when I heard that distinctive yell. It was the same
screeching noise I remembered hearing in Scotland, and I
waited with bated breath. It was answered.

Presently they came and at first I thought they looked like
two German Shepherd dogs. This breed is beautiful and
has a characteristic gait when working sheep, creeping
along with the belly almost touching the ground and tail flat
out behind.

But their heads were entirely different, big blunt heads in
fact, and short tails, bigger than normal cats but certainly
not more than 3 ft over-all. They were quite close but I
could not tell their colour, and they attacked a fresh oxhead
as if starving—though they looked well fed.

These were wild descendants of domestic cats. They
grow bigger heads and shorter tails than tame cats and are
also said to be untameable.

Before the war when gamekeepers were plentiful the cats
hardly existed because they ate a lot of game and were
regarded as a pest. But there are no gamekeepers here now
and no game so we don't bother about them.

These two made their efficient meal and departed happily in about five minutes, never having noticed me.

*   *   *

Winter is generally not the time to repair fences, but a warm
and sunny spell the other day seemed the perfect oppor-
tunity to break this rule of thumb.

So, with a few stakes, a post, a roll of smooth wire (I never
use barbed wire) and fencing tools, I went off to the bottom
paddock and settled down to a couple of hours' toil under a
watery sun.

Our eastern boundary, where I was working, is on the
edge of a very swampy piece of land which once belonged
to this farm. Sadly, over the years, previous owners of the
farm had disposed of it and other bits of their land.

From a 25-acre smallholding on which a small family
could just about make a living, it eventually had only five
acres left. Twenty had been sold off and I bought what was

left for a song—with a good Land-Rover thrown in. We have never regretted the purchase.

The swamp was bought by a forestry company which planted it with larch and Sitka spruce, the only kind of agriculture for which it is any use. And at present that little forest is at its most fascinating.

The conifers have not yet attained enough height to kill off the native scrub with which the land has always been covered; here and there are patches of heather, blackberry thickets and on all the banks where the sun catches them, blueberries.

Gorse, broom and bracken abound along with the odd rowan and a fascinating profusion of native wildflowers, including orchids. But these are not expensive beauties like the orchids of Latin America, that cost the earth and are parasites living on tall trees in the steaming tropical jungles.

Our Welsh orchids are tiny things, have no market value as far as I know, and do not harbour virulently poisonous snakes. But they are beautiful.

This also happens to be the abode of our marsh-tits, regular customers at our bird-table, though since the fickle weather turned warmer they have not been there so often.

Anyway, there I was, laying out my stakes and starting the process of hammering out holes for them with a heavy sledgehammer and a thick crowbar. This made a lot of noise but, on looking up to take a breather, I saw I had an attentive audience. The noise did not disturb them at all and before I had taken three deep breaths they were all around me investigating my stake hole.

Could there be anything in it to eat? Had I been turning up worms, wireworms, leatherjackets or any of the many creepy-crawlies that inhabit such crannies? Certainly not, but how could I disappoint those poor little stomachs?

Fortunately, as the weather was clement I had taken my lunch. So, putting my cushion atop the bank in the sun, I produced my sandwiches.

They were good ones made with wholemeal bread baked the previous day. I opened up one and laid the two pieces down between my feet.

Immediately each slice was covered with six tits. Since

there were more than a dozen waiting impatiently, I put another one down. Before the third had been offered there must have been nearly 30 marsh-tits and by this time I had another half dozen prospecting my boots. I had to make do with a warming drink out of my flask, which refreshed me sufficiently to finish the job and tidy up nicely.

Then I went up to the house accompanied by at least a dozen marsh-tits. There they were able to fill in the crannies from a large lump of fat and a red net bag of peanuts hanging from the nearest blackthorn.

* * *

Our dry-stone wall forms the dividing line between the top (forecourt) and bottom (New Garden) parts of what we call our small-bird table.

Voles live safely inside that wall and may often be seen feeding when the small birds are doing likewise.

They seem to live very amicably together though the voles, the most cuddly little creatures of their size anywhere to be found (and so easy to tame, too) are well equipped to fight for their food if necessary.

Indeed, in the years since we first saw that voles had taken up their abode in the wall, there has only been one occasion when friction occurred, and that was during a very cold spell.

As is well known, when it is extremely cold at night, tits tend to crowd up together in any old hole in any old masonry for the night, so as to generate a warming fug to keep life in their tiny bodies.

Well, late one afternoon when the temperature had already dropped to minus three or four Centigrade—and could be guaranteed to drop as much again before next morning—an adventurous blue tit discovered a small hole in the wall leading to what must have been quite a large cavity. And in less than no time three more tits were excitedly popping in and out of it.

Then, as my wife and I watched, fascinated, from the living-room window, two voles appeared side by side in that hole in the wall, determined to repel the invaders.

The first tit to attack was roughly forced back and several feathers fluttered to the ground; a second tit followed the first and a few more feathers were lost in the fray.

But then the tits varied their tactics. For two flying tits to attack at once would have been impossible because the inner wings would have got tangled up and both birds would momentarily have their vulnerable throats left open to those vicious rodent teeth.

So another tit began quietly climbing down through a hole from above, obviously planning to spear the shrews with his lethally sharp beak, while his friends continued fluttering and cursing outside the hole.

However, my wife intervened to prevent such a deadly solution to the territorial dispute. She let out an ear-splitting yell and the tits immediately flew off. The two little defenders, without so much as a thank-you glance in our direction, likewise made themselves scarce.

My wife then jammed a stone into that hole, knowing there were plenty of other smaller ones big enough for the voles to squeeze through but too small for the tits. And there has not been any similar trouble since.

But three or four days ago my wife reported that there was a pregnant vole behind the big cornbin in the little granary backing on to the donkey's loosebox.

Now, since tits took up residence in the stable wall, we have previously had nothing but long-tailed fieldmice in that granary. The voles already had ample accommodation in the dry-stone wall, with an abundance of food. So why should this one decide to move?

The only reason I can think of is that the wall between the looseboxes, with a horse on one side and two donkeys on the other, is much warmer.

Could the little creature's instinct be telling her that there could really be a *really* cold snap coming up in the next day or two?

* * *

After a few days away last week I am so glad to be home with all my friends again.

The dogs Holly and Teena were the first to greet me, shoving their heads into my hands to say how glad they were that I was back, particularly as I hadn't forgotten to bring them a titbit or two.

After a warming drink in the house I went back out again to see Patchy, my wife's gelding, who was glad to bury his nose in half a bucket of sugarbeet flakes that had been seasoned with a mugful of warmed molasses, which he loves.

Geese and chickens were then attended to with a bigger-than-ordinary feed on the forecourt and both peanut-carriers were loaded for the tits.

Incidentally, all the bantams are in lay and while we watched them an enormous buzzard flew slowly over the house with a large stick across his beak, obviously for building or repairing a nest. They all seem to think that after a few dry, sunny days spring has finally come. I do hope they're right and that we are not in the lull before a final horrible snow-up.

However, within five minutes two buzzards returned to settle on our field of skulls where something had already been put out for them and the other carrion birds that feed there.

After we returned to the house two robins arrived on the window-sill asking for something. As my wife opened the window and put out a handful of corn, they were immediately joined by two dunnocks, charming, but not at all pushful, little birds.

The pushful ones were not to be denied. As it was a warm day my wife left one window open, and in flew a tomtit as they always will.

He made a skilful round of the room, noticing a few crumbs around a plate from which I had just eaten a couple of bloater-paste sandwiches. He quickly polished them off and flew out again and I sat back thankfully. I was home again. . . .

*   *   *

People often ask me about the "cows' cornflakes" I mention

for feeding birds. And it could be that your local pet shop man will hoot with laughter when you ask for them. If so, go to a corn chandler and ask for flaked maize.

He will give it to you, and you could find it to be a most versatile food. Why, I have even eaten it myself for breakfast and found it perfectly palatable.

Many sheep farmers use it as the main ingredient for a sheepdog food in winter because it is packed with calories, which means instant heat and strength in hard times. We use it for our bantams as well as our small-bird horde. And although we always provide it mixed with other food, it is the flaked maize that both wild birds and bantams go for first.

The bigger wild birds—from thrush up—can easily swallow an entire flake, but the smaller ones break up each flake and eat the bits. When you get down to wren size, those little bits are broken up smaller still until the human eye would need a magnifying glass to see them.

Speaking of wrens (and we have three pairs around our cottage) I have an old nature book which says: "Down in the underwood the tail-up wrens are hopping from one eligible building site to another, finding it difficult to choose; for that beautiful domed nest must be hidden so that nobody can find it. Then—the nest half finished —jenny wren drops a thread of grass with a scream and turns pale. Somebody has touched it; a shred of grass has been moved half a hair's-breadth, and nothing will induce the pair to touch the nest again. They find another place and, with luck, build a new nest without being discovered."

Too bad. Poor little things. But up here those beautiful and so carefully made domed edifices with a doorway in the side have not existed since the first woad-clad native Welsh started to build their dry-stone walls.

Those Welshmen knew that little wrens were valuable killers of all kinds of nasty little creepy-crawlies and needed looking after. So in those dry-stone walls they left little dome-shaped holes here and there, with tiny little round entrances. And those holes have served as cosy homes for the wrens ever since.

We have one wall that is only about 20 paces long but is between five and six feet thick all along, presumably because the makers wanted to plant ash trees along it. In fact three strong ash trees are still there, past their best perhaps but still stoutly withstanding the worst winds that can blow.

And inside the wall live our little wrens which we feed twice a day on their own little bird-table along the wall, which is near the front of the house. And whenever my wife or I comes near, they do not drop everything and disappear, but just go on with whatever they happen to be doing, which for the last three days has been nest-repairing.

We have been watching them take little bits of hay, scraps of sheep wool off barbed wire fences and so forth into their holes in the wall . . . when they have not been too busy guzzling down all the flaked maize that we put out for them, that is.

*   *   *

When they asked me down in the village to forecast the weather for the next few days I told them, more or less in jest, to get ready for snow.

And, by golly, that's exactly what we got: five inches of it on the level, accompanied by a rapid drop of the glass.

Now there's a very mild thaw and if anyone asks me about the weather again I need only to point at our two peanut cages, both visible from the living-room; one right over the window, the other just opposite in the first blackthorn.

From dawn's early light to dusk they are packed with all our usual brands of tit: great tits and tomtits, marsh-tits and coal tits—plus dunnocks and treecreepers. And all of them eating so fast that both cages have to be filled twice a day—and they are big cages.

Tits are highly intelligent birds and obviously they are filling up with as much protein and calories as they can because they expect more cold to come.

Feathered predators that frequent the skull paddock

have been feeding hungrily, too. These are mostly members of the crow family, and include just one jay, a singleton who lost his mate at least two years ago.

We believe him to be a cock bird and he keeps very much to himself but always calls an amiable greeting to my wife or myself during his feeding times in the paddock.

However, he objects strongly to the presence of any quadruped predators such as badgers, martens, polecats and foxes.

The only time I have ever seen him at a disadvantage was when he tackled a big hedgehog and two of her young ones (already well grown) last year. He descended on them with his usual loud squawks and Hammer film monster sounds but they just looked up at him in the rather static way of hedgehogs, and went on eating.

Whereupon our jay swooped to the attack and got a mouthful of prickles.

Having recovered from this, he approached on foot for a fresh attack but what did he see? Nothing but three perfect spheres of prickles. Prickles in every direction.

He cautiously tested one but gave up and took wing to his own oxhead, in silence.

He doesn't go for badgers or foxes either because both species are big and battle-wise. He just yells at them from a respectable distance until, maddened by the noise, like I am at modern pop music, they quietly depart.

That is why the jay used to be a favourite bird of the gamekeepers. They always liked one or two in every covert because if anything nasty like a fox or a two-legged poacher came into his bailiwick the resident jay would awaken whatever the hour of night and give his raucous warning, alerting the gamekeeper, who would thereupon issue forth with his gun.

March

Here in wild Welsh mountain country we must be coming to the end of the most extreme blow-warm-blow-cold winter I can remember in the past 20 years or so and all our stock is in much finer fettle than I'd have expected.

We have only seven hens (plus Cocky Olly), which are more than keeping the two of us in eggs. This is amazing, particularly as they seem to have gone off their laying pellets since we started varying their diet with a 50–50 mix of cows' cornflakes and mixed corn.

However, everyone likes a change now and then, including my wife who is threatening to get some Khaki-Campbell ducks, so that we can use their eggs for cake-making.

The trouble is that she wants to make a duck-pond in the Old Garden. This will be picturesque but is going to cost a bit. On the other hand, neither of us being gardeners it will cure our feeling of guilt at never having put spade to that garden during the past few years.

As for our quadruped stock, Patchy, my wife's skewbald gelding, is well and winter-fat. In really cold weather he keeps warm by having an all-over roll in fresh mud every few days, then moving about briskly until it dries. This leaves him with a windproof coat.

The only snag about this is that if my wife wants to saddle him up to go somewhere where even the Land-Rover won't go, it takes a couple of hours of hard grooming to get him in a fit state to be seen under a saddle anywhere—even on our single-track mountain roads. So we are not fussy.

Our two donkeys, Rebecca and her daughter, Naomi, both get daily rations of corn and as much hay as they need.

So they are also fat and healthy. Unlike Patchy, they grow mammoth-like winter coats and therefore need no mud great-coats and are always more or less clean.

The other day we were keeping warm in the living-room with the wood fire burning bright to the accompaniment of two oil fires and one pressure lamp. It was a bitterly cold afternoon with an icy wind blasting down from the north-east, giving us a taste of the Arctic Barents Sea. Suddenly Rebecca's anguished bray shook the window and there was her frantic nose trying to push a pane in.

We rushed out to see Naomi stuck fast halfway through the boundary fence quite near the house.

Pausing only to grab a wire cutter from my work room I followed my wife to the filly who was obviously in great discomfort.

She had one small hoof stuck through the sheep-netting and a couple of quick snips would have cleared it if she had given me time to pull it back. Not at all; with one quick thrust she rammed her leg further in so that she was now held fast above the knee.

This meant cutting the netting from top to bottom. By this time Naomi had fallen over and was struggling in panic.

My wife and I pulled her clear and she fell down the bank on which the fence is built.

Brushing the mud off our hands we waited until she had got up, expecting her to rush to Rebecca for a comforting drink. But—and there's gratitude for you!—with her ears flat back, she emitted what can only be described as an infuriated snarl, leaped towards me in reverse and caught me with a sharp kick above the knee.

Fortunately it did not hurt much as I had time to jump back, missing the main force of the blow.

Only then did Naomi go to her mum for comfort . . . and I went to work repairing the sheep-netting while my wife returned to the house to make us a well deserved cup of tea.

* * *

Gale-force winds from the south-east early in the week, with a shattering thunderstorm accompanied by hail, made me wonder if we may be in for a final cold spell before the end of the month.

Alternative high and low pressure areas have been racing in succession across the Atlantic, and I hope this does not mean that something nasty is beginning to boil up in the Barents Sea, far away to the north-east.

Be that as it may, a little warmth has been noticeable to bird, beast and humankind here. Indeed, one of our friends proudly told us a few days ago that he had already discarded his winter woollies and looked astounded when my wife remarked that we seldom discard ours until the first week in June.

The bird-table is always a good weather indicator. Quite accidentally it seems, we occasionally get a warm and sunny day in January and February and on such days we are deserted by chaffinches, blackbirds and thrushes.

This has happened on about six days altogether this year. But we are never deserted by our resident tits in three varieties and, of course, all the predatory birds and beasts that strip the oxheads we put down for them in the skull paddock.

Two grey squirrels which turned up one day about a fortnight ago, in an appalling state of emaciation, and wolfed all that they could on the forecourt bird-table, have become permanent residents.

After several days they transferred their activities to the skull paddock but we never realised how much they had improved until the day before yesterday when they brought a poor relation in.

Like the first two, this one arrived as practically a walking skeleton. And he attacked the food exactly as the other two had done on their first day, wolfing it down like a starving cow, on all fours with head down.

By this time the other two had shining coats and plenty of flesh underneath; not only that, but they had resumed the standard manners of nearly all rodents. That is to say, they were sitting up as though at table, cutting a piece of meat off with their rodent teeth, then holding it in their hands, washing their noses and whiskers after the meal.

None of that for this poor newcomer. He just gorged until

he could eat no more, then walked off, his belly dragging on the ground, to have a drink at the stream. He was followed by his two fat and shining friends, doubtless making snide asides to each other.

Now, after only three days, the third one is beginning to get a gloss on his coat and doubtless he'll soon be as sleek and as dainty a feeder as the others.

* * *

The other day my wife drove off to a nearby farm to buy a goat—quite a step for us to take because we haven't kept any since we moved to this smallholding.

The reason for this is that goats can be tiresome creatures, especially to gardeners, unless they are properly fenced in.

We decided, though, that the benefits of having our own independent milk supply would outweigh any disadvantages, particularly as we intend doing some landscaping that will involve fencing off what we call the Old Garden.

We shall make a hole in the wall between the Old Garden and the small west paddock, thus leaving both for geese, ducks and goat.

This plan will not only keep a goat away from our proper garden but will also stop the geese making such a mess of the forecourt.

I awaited my wife's return with great hopes and as soon as I heard the car return I rushed out to see what it contained.

To my amazement there were two goats, comfortably cuddled up in the back. One of them was the little white yearling for which my wife had paid £3.75, but the other was full-grown, a most beautiful Nubian nanny with ears down to her knees like Snoopy. She was obviously worth far more than the yearling and I wondered what my bank manager was going to say. Very quickly, before I had a chance to explode, my wife explained.

The seller's farm was too small for the number of animals it carried. So she was reducing her stock. And as this goat was a very affectionate creature she was throwing her in for free as she knew she would be appreciated here.

And so, of course, she will. For as soon as I opened the back door of the car out she bounced and jumped up to put both her feet into my hands and give me loving nibbles all over my face.

Her name was Alice. So we called the little white one Amy and brought them in for a welcome drink, or in their case a handful of crushed maize with a spoonful of molasses to sweeten it, while we sipped a sherry.

Then we showed them to their temporary quarters and left them happily bedded down in some straw.

*   *   *

Over the last ten days, believe it or not, the barometer has twice risen and fallen by a full inch, each time in the space of 24 hours.

Day temperatures have varied from freezing up to the high forties Fahrenheit, and night temperatures have gone from far below freezing to normal spring temperatures.

Up here, when in a quandary about the weather, I pay particular attention to what the animals are doing.

First of all, the badgers. On the morning following a deep frost, while everything was still hoared over, I saw them down at the bottom of the skull paddock—and they were there for quite a while, around a fresh skull my wife had put there the previous evening.

Since then they have made no more broad-daylight forays, but have visited us early in the night or early in the morning. This means that they are by no means in deep hibernation but are behaving as they do in early spring.

Now for the poultry, if that's the right expression for a mixture of geese and bantams. If not, they have my apologies.

The day before the barometer started to go mad, our goose Vicky, to our immense surprise, produced her first egg. After seeing her with her mate Albert, investigating the haybay, my wife went over to see what was going on. Ten minutes later she returned with the news that Albert was supervising Vicky in the building of her first nest.

The usual untidy affair thus looked as though a small

cyclone had deposited a rough circle of hay on the cement floor. Now and again Albert, with lordly *sotto voce* quacking, would carefully pick up a strand of hay and deposit it somewhere else. One he discarded altogether, although my wife couldn't see anything wrong with it and carefully tucked it back when Albert wasn't looking.

Since then, Vicky has produced another, every 48 hours, despite thunderstorms, hail, sleet and snow. Every other day at nine o'clock, we see Albert doing his proud goose-step outside the haybay door and know that Vicky is doing her job on the nest.

It is amazing how he looks after her, never letting her get more than five yards away from him, washing her and preening her until I marvel that she has a feather left. But on the contrary, she is both larger and more beautiful than when she first came.

Now, if they're down at paddock bottom and we want them, all either of us has to do is to call "come along, quack-quack" four or five times in quick succession and they, after the ritual polite reply, come belting up at full speed and fully vocal.

As for the bantams, they have been laying for quite a while, and have held to the same production rate all through this crazy spell.

Bless them all, geese, badgers and bantams.

*　　*　　*

My wife noticed it first. She came rushing in from feeding the chickens and small birds on the forecourt to announce rather breathlessly that five-foot flames and clouds of smoke were shooting out of our chimney.

I ran outside and saw that the fire was even more serious than that. For smoke was also curling out from the eaves at the end of the house, which meant that the blaze had spread to one of the roof-beams, putting the whole roof in danger.

I quickly got one of our four big fire-extinguishers going, pointing it straight up the vast chimney. The house was

built early in the eighteenth century when they made even
cottage chimneys wide enough for a ten or 12-year-old boy
to climb up, with little footholes on the sides to make the
climbing easier.

I had never thought it possible that such a wide flue could
possibly soot up to danger-point, particularly as we supple-
ment our wood supply with coal only when temperatures
go below zero.

I had now been proved wrong. But the fire extinguisher
seemed to have extinguished all the noise of roaring flame
and I was sure it had reached right to the top. Wrong again.
By the time I got outside again I saw that there was still at
least two feet of rising flame.

This was the moment to dial 999—the first time I have
ever had to do so. By now the forecourt had filled up with
neighbours. The nearest live half a mile away by road but
you can see a long way in the hills. And one of them told me
he had already rung the fire brigade because he knew that
although our chimneys would last for many years without
cleaning, if they did catch fire it could be very dangerous
indeed because the great heat could destroy the mortar,
causing them to collapse.

But as he was telling me this the fire engine roared into
the forecourt and the fire was put out in next to no time.

Inside, three firemen had rolled back the carpet and
moved furniture well away from the fireplace where vast
lumps of incandescent soot were being shovelled into
buckets and carried away. Within a couple of hours the
drama was over, and a new fire was burning merrily in the
grate.

Now, the most remarkable aspect of all this (except the
speed with which the firemen handled what could have
been a most expensive fire) was the conduct of the dogs.
From the time my wife had raised the alarm, they hadn't
made a sound. They just left the house and in spite of the
smoke, the milling neighbours and the arrival of the fire-
engine they gave not a bark or a growl between them. In
fact they behaved themselves perfectly—and seemed to
know perfectly what it was all about.

So we have to give thanks for our efficient firemen, the

best of neighbours—and the most sensible of dogs in an emergency.

*   *   *

During the past week we have had some really spring-like weather, excellent for walking the dogs, even if the nights continue frosty.

Yesterday morning's walk took us through a particularly low-level patch of conifer forest to a place where the dogs nearly always get a run—a natural rocky clearing alongside a river where there is too little soil to hold the shallow roots of even a Sitka spruce, the commonest type of conifer used by the planters in Wales.

The clearing, consisting of about half an acre of bramble, bracken and other kinds of weed, has been taken over by a community of rabbits, which generally do very well there.

Suddenly Teena our Jack Russell, who had run on ahead, started to give tongue wildly and Holly the Rottweiler, who had been walking alongside my wife, dashed off to see what was up. Within a few seconds her voice was added to Teena's. So we hurried on at full speed. And there, lying struggling in a deep tractor-rut, lay a large milky doe rabbit with two tiny young ones crouching against her, both rigid with terror.

Calling the dogs off and slipping a chain over each neck, my wife got the dogs out of the way and stood back with them for me to make an examination. The cause was easy to identify—the tag-end of a lead-weighted couple of feet of nylon fishing-line which must have been discarded by an angler.

The rabbit had entangled herself by stepping on it and had we arrived, say, ten minutes later, the story would have ended with one dead doe and two doomed babies.

I got to work with my pocket-knife and in half a minute she was free but, possibly from fear, as yet quite helpless. So my wife went ahead with the dogs (who were very reluctant to leave) while I walked on a few yards to the nearest tree and hid behind it.

For about ten minutes they remained motionless. Then a

car went by, on the nearby but out-of-sight road, and the
doe pulled herself together, got up on three sound feet and
started limping along a rut towards a bramble thicket on the
highest part of the clearing.

At first she had trouble with her babies who wanted to
travel in the rut alongside her, but there wasn't room for
three abreast. So she got them both in front of her and
pushed them along with her nose. And so the little family
vanished into safety and I rejoined my wife.

*   *   *

It was not that we weren't ready to provide for our two new
goats when they arrived. Just that the weather wasn't.

Not yet having a goat-proof enclosure, the only way they
could safely graze would be to stake them out. Stakes, lines
and collars—everything was ready except for the fact that
nowhere on this smallholding is there sufficient grass.

Our last snow-up was followed by a string of bitterly cold
nights with dry daytime winds. This dried out what small
amount of grass there was.

Naturally the goats are on hard feed. They have it twice a
day in the disused chicken-pen which is dry and weatherproof. Here too they get their hay-ration. But that's not
enough to keep them either happy or healthy.

Thank heavens, therefore, for the verges on the lanes. Up
to 60 years ago, before the days of mechanical transport for
sheep and cattle, the verges never got a chance to grow.
When animals went to market, professional drovers took
them considerable distances by road to railhead, sometimes
up to 50 miles or more.

As they ambled along they grazed what they could along
the verges until they came to a drovers' resting place such
as the Rovers' Rest or Rovers' Return, where they spent the
night in one of the small paddocks surrounding the pub.
Then on next day.

But all that ended with the advent of horse-boxes and
cattle-and-sheep lorries and now the verges—except after
the twice-yearly county-council trim-up—are luxuriantly
grassed all the year round.

So there we were the morning after the goats arrived, my wife holding on to Alice, the beautiful Nubian nanny, with a dog lead on her collar, while I was looking after Amy, the yearling Saanen. They were both gobbling away happily when a car came by driven by a friend, who slowed down to have a word with us. As the car approached both goats stepped on to the verge and went on grazing.

Then Amy, seeing a nearby mudguard, turned and went to scratch her pretty head on it. Whereupon Alice officiously went over and butted her away back to the safety of the verge.

We continued our grazing and that was the last time we bothered about dog-leads. Those sensible little animals keep quite close to us and come to heel without any orders whenever a horseless carriage passes by.

*   *   *

We have had our heaviest snowfall of this winter and are still in its cold white grip without, so it would seem, much chance of a change for the next few days.

When I awoke the other morning it was still pitch dark and bitterly cold in the bedroom. So I got up without waking my wife and dressed to get the banked fire going and tea.

But first I went outside to check the temperature. The sky was clear, there was not a breath of wind, and the thermometer said minus seven Centigrade. And as we had not reached the coldest hour, which is just before dawn, I knew I could expect a drop of at least two more degrees before sunrise.

Very soon the fire was burning bright and the room began to warm up nicely. With my first mug of tea I began to warm up too, and by the time the eastern horizon began to show up as a thin strip of light I went outside again.

It was then that I heard a sort of grunt in the paddock where I put oxheads to feed predatory birds. So I flashed my powerful torch in that direction and saw three badgers scampering away down the hill.

I decided to go down there to see what the badgers had

been up to, and I had to walk rather gingerly because there was still a good foot of snow and the surface was frozen hard.

When I reached the spot I saw to my amazement that these badgers had cleared the snow off the six freshest oxheads, two of which happened to be from very young beasts, and had been able to get at the brains.

The badgers had also saved me a job. For I had intended to go down later on when the sun came out—if it did not cloud over as it often does around sunrise—to clear the snow away from those same skulls.

Good for them, I thought. Now, not only had they had a nice breakfast, but done me a good turn into the bargain; paying for their meal, as it were.

Soon the sun was coming up over the hills and presently all our local ravens, carrion crows, a few jackdaws and the usual team of magpies were all over the oxheads enjoying a good breakfast.

Then I saw something my wife had reported seeing two days previously. Suddenly three ravens set upon a smaller bird, which flew fast up to the forecourt on to the large patch from which the snow had been cleared, where I had just put down the first small-bird breakfast.

My wife had described it exactly; it was the same length as a jackdaw but chunkier in build. It had the very shiny jet-black beak that the ravens and carrion crows possess. It had no grey on its neck as jackdaws have and was also not a rook because these birds (which always nest in a communal rookery) have as their distinguishing mark a dirty grey ring around the base of the beak.

It was obviously fully fledged and I concluded (as I had after my wife's description) that it could only be the runt of a raven or a crow's last year's brood and was regarded as an outsider by others of its breed. However, this very neat mini-raven or crow was extremely well-mannered on the table, molesting none of the smaller birds, but just pecking happily away on flaked maize and pullet-pellets.

*　　　*　　　*

At midnight, when I took my last look out of doors, the thermometer showed four degrees of frost, while in the morning, when the sun was shining directly on the thermometer, it had reached 2 degrees Centigrade.

I hope and pray for an early summer with plenty of sun, but on making that remark in our local I was warned that what we get one end of the year we have to pay for at the other. So it is better just to take what comes and be thankful for it, whatever it may be.

Be that as it may, at mid-day the next day there was a cold bright sun in a cold blue sky as I looked out at the masses of chilled birds feeding away as hard as they could on the various bird-tables around the place.

As usual in such weather, their feathers were fluffed out to make them look twice their normal size and, let's hope, to make them feel twice as warm, poor things.

Suddenly a cloud of small birds arose from the forecourt where they had been feeding and took shelter in nearby trees and bushes.

And there in the middle of the dry and snowless patch of concrete was a half-breed sheepdog busy scrabbling up the odd cornflake amidst various different kinds of seed. Indeed, it was behaving like a half-starved animal and was certainly in a miserable condition.

I was just thinking of putting on a bit of extra clothing and going out to investigate when I heard our own dogs, which my wife had taken for a walk, approaching the cottage. They came trotting down the hill for home, looking forward to settling down near the fire with a biscuit or two to warm them, then shot through the gateway as my wife came panting round the corner close behind.

Then it was that they saw the strange dog. And before I could act they took off after him, emitting murderous yells.

Away he went with a pitiful yap of terror, straight down the paddock of the skulls where several buzzards and ravens, which had been peacefully feeding, immediately took part in the attack. That poor dog only just managed to clear the bottom fence, but by that time my wife was in the picture and blowing the recall on her whistle.

Thankfully the dogs obeyed her and, with a final defiant

bark or two, turned back to come trotting up to the cottage.

It was impossible now for us to catch that terrified sheepdog. So we could but hope that he had gone home or would find someone to care for him.

*   *   *

Never in my life before have I know such a piece of weather: a two-minute mini-hurricane it was, catching us unawares as we drove into town.

At the top of a steep little hill we suddenly spotted a mating battle between two buck hares. As usual we did not see the doe, doubtless well hidden out of the wind.

The battle was most uneven. I don't know how long it had been going on but after a minute the end was obvious. The smaller of the two was losing fast and finally a double-footed kick shot him quite high into the teeth of the wind. He came down on the spot he had left.

The victor jumped up onto a small rocky outcrop to do his triumphant victory dance for the benefit of the watching doe.

But alas, hare proposes, God disposes. When the victor had gained maximum height on his first Nijinsky-type leap, there came a better-than-Storm-Force gust.

Down he came, at least six feet nearer to us, tumbling sideways over and over. Almost at the speed of light he arrived at the bottom with an audible bang into the trunk of a stout beech tree, to lie there half-stunned, breathing like a blacksmith's bellows.

The vanquished one by this time was visible again, looking towards the victor. Had he won the fight? Obviously the answer was Yes, at least in his book.

He looked to where the doe's head was now just visible. And it was clear that she shared his opinion. For as he hopped gaily forward, they touched noses before he had started his second jump, and side by side they went on their happy way.

*   *   *

As far as the hundreds of birds which use our so-called "bird-table" throughout the year are concerned, spring has come at last.

They have been singing their spring song at the top of their voices ever since last Sunday. Not only that: our two pairs of blackbirds are busy making their nests and so are the robins.

The chaffinches appear to be mating, noisily as is their wont. The tits, no doubt busy doing up their nests, are not much in view except early in the morning when the first food is put out, and again at about sundown.

As to the ravens that nest here, they are repairing the old squirrel-drey that they occupied after their first winter here five years ago. Since then they have raised four broods, all of which have built nests within a quarter of a mile—some of them much nearer—of their winter food supply.

But if spring really is here, our trees and undergrowth are taking no notice. Which may mean much colder weather to come, perhaps even snow which, leaving a covering over bare or wind-swept ground, is much warmer than deep frosts—particularly at this time of year.

There's not a green leaf nor even a fat bud showing yet. And still no sign of any forthcoming beech-mast or hazel-nut crop.

If there is none it will be the fourth year running that this has happened at our level above the sea—about 900 ft to 1100 ft—and the effects could be serious for our squirrels, particularly our native red ones.

This past week we have been digging out a goose-and-duck-pond in the Old Garden.

I've always called it the Old Garden because, although only about 45 ft by 55 ft in size, it is a maze of little footpaths, all lined with white quartz rocks with what was obviously loving care between 100 and 200 years ago by the little old lady we have sometimes seen standing in front of the antique Ironbridge cooking range in our living-room.

She is tiny and smaller than my wife. When she appears it is always in the same place, on the left-hand side of the fireplace. She warms her hands at that old range which she may have helped to install something like 150 years ago. She obviously loves it and we welcome her.

There is only four to six inches of topsoil on a clay foundation and therefore can only have been used for light-rooted flowers and plants. At any rate, we do know that blackcurrant bushes flourish there, and also any kind of winter bulb or the ordinary cottage flowers such as sweet william or night-scented stock.

But the interesting thing about our half-finished pond, in which water has already collected, is that after only four days' work on it a colony of those insects known as water-boatmen has already settled down there, its members keeping themselves busy using their legs to row all over the place.

* * *

Since Christmas-time we have had some of the harshest weather I can remember. Yet our little Christmas tree, which I threw out on the Twelfth Night at the stroke of midnight, is still alive.

This is amazing because though its roots have been encased in a plastic pot, the tree has been lying on its side on the dry-stone wall we have been gradually extending during the past few years.

The only apparent effect of being out there in the snow, torrential rain and temperatures as low as minus 6C is a slight browning at the top. But the tree—a locally grown Sitka spruce—has not shed a single needle.

If I had thought three months ago that the tree had a chance of survival I would not, of course, have treated it in such a callous fashion. But a friend had assured me that it would die because I had cut off the top eight inches (otherwise it would have been too tall for our low-ceilinged living-room).

Well, the other day I decided nothing would be lost if I planted it out in what we call the New Garden, near the dry-stone wall (not that it is really a garden at all in the proper sense. For neither my wife nor I can remotely be described as gardeners).

I dug a hole and mixed into the soil some plant food that seems to have worked wonders for the old rambling rose at the front of our house. And when I took the tree out of its pot I saw that already it was growing new, twisting little roots which means that, even with its top missing, it will survive.

I felt well pleased with my work and when my wife returned from a walk with the dogs she was equally pleased to see the little tree standing there so prettily.

But the very next morning, that tree was in danger. I had got up early and looked out of the bedroom window in the half-light of early dawn to see a wild polecat next to it. These creatures, like their near relations the stoat, ferret and the much rarer pine marten, are carnivorous but at certain times of the year are apt to behave like squirrels and eat away the bark of young conifers, killing them.

Obviously, I couldn't allow this to happen here. So I tip-toed downstairs, got my 12-bore shotgun, loaded it, crept back upstairs, opened the window and . . . *BANG!*

I had aimed to miss the polecat by a foot or so and it was quite unharmed. But it had the shock of its life and was off like a bat out of hell.

So that little creature will never return. And I don't expect to see his friends here either. For when danger lurks, such clever little beasts soon pass the word around.

April

The other night, two days after my wife had seen the first bat of the year, I saw a couple of the little creatures fluttering around the hospitality light which illuminates the entire forecourt beautifully.

And fluttering even closer to the lamp's 100 watt bulb, frequently bumping right into it, were a cluster of moths.

The bats were of our smallest resident species, the pipistrelle. They were not going for the bigger moths but were feasting upon the smaller ones at the rate of two or three a minute.

After a few minutes they vanished into the granary at the far end of the house, passing not more than two feet above my head as I stood in the middle of the yard.

Then my wife joined me and within half a minute another bat came into the circle of light. At first I thought it was a Natterer's Bat, which is both gregarious and squeaky. But I soon realised it was in fact a Whiskered Bat, which hunts in silence and often in solitude—like this one.

It appeared to be the same size as the little recently-departed pipistrelles but with a different type of flight, and we watched it enjoy several minutes of quite good hunting. But then it had a nasty accident which, but for our presence, would have proved fatal.

Suddenly it banged loudly up against the thick glass globe surrounding the light and fell 12 feet straight down into the middle of the rainwater barrel between the end of the house and the garage.

Now two or three years ago we discovered a dead bat in this barrel which had evidently had the same kind of accident. Had the barrel been full, it could quite possibly have got out over the rim. But on that occasion there had only been about six inches of water.

Now the barrel was full to overflowing but even so we hurried to it to give the bat a hand.

It was lying on its back, floating high in the water but apparently quite knocked out when my wife picked it up. We took the little thing indoors and laid it on a nice dry, absorbent newspaper. Within five minutes it had recovered and when I put my hand in its path, it climbed up onto it and stayed there, possibly liking the warmth.

I took it outside where I tossed it up, and away it flew.

*   *   *

Though it has long been the custom to put a ring in a pig's nose, a lot of townspeople wonder why.

Certainly a ring is put in a bull's nose because this is one of the most sensitive parts of his body and is therefore a good place to hook on his lead rope.

But surely, I can hear townies muttering, a pig is not as powerful as a bull? Well, under certain circumstances that is debatable, though being able to lead a pig is not the main reason for ringing the animal's nose.

The fact is that a pig's nose is not just used for breathing and smelling. It is not nearly as sensitive to pain as the nose of a bull, but it is a very sensitive smeller which can identify and locate roots and other delicacies such as truffles.

Then it becomes an extremely efficient ploughshare that never needs sharpening, that will dig as deep as necessary. The result, in a field, can be squalid—because a pig doesn't plough in a tidy way as we do, but all over the place, wherever it smells anything edible.

But, put an iron ring through its nose and it makes ploughing not only uncomfortable, but even painful.

Which brings me to the day some months ago when we were stopped on our way into our market town by an enormous sow lying flat across the middle of the road. She was so big that she seemed to extend from verge to verge. And all along her belly was a double line of tiny piglets, each one attached to a tap.

I stopped and hooted one gentle toot. The sow answered with two polite and gentle honks and heaved herself laboriously to all fours.

Herding her family to the verge, she waited for us to pass. Then the whole lot returned to the same spot—already nicely warmed—and resumed operations.

Time passed. Then, going in to town one day last week, we came on an amazing scene. There was not a pig in sight but the road was littered with big and little clods of earth that the pigs—now much bigger and weaned—had, in their search for roots, ploughed from the verges under the supervision of the loving sow.

On the way home we came across the whole gang on a blind corner and had to brake hard. There seemed to be about 50—all busily engaged ploughing clods on to the road—but a quick count revealed that there were no more than 15.

They appeared quite pleased to see us and when my wife got out to act as a red flagman, they crowded round her as though expecting her to get down on all fours and begin rooting about greedily with her own snout.

Eventually we got out on the other side, honked a sweet farewell on the horn and were answered by a noisy chorus of 15 songsters.

*   *   *

We have now finished digging out the goose-pond in what we call the Old Garden and are well pleased with the result.

The pond is about 12 ft across at its widest point, 5 or 6 ft at the shortest and nowhere deeper than about 2½ ft.

As it is fed by a rollicking little mountain stream which carries a lot of mud, there is already about a foot of sediment in the middle. And by the time Albert and Vicky have completed their morning ablutions there, you can't see more than an inch into the water—if that.

When the geese are not about I've stood entranced, watching the antics of about half a dozen water-boatmen, those big beetles with long hind legs that row themselves at great speed in any water that is deep enough. They are fascinating creatures and where the stream enters the pool they have to scoot furiously in the fast-moving water.

While the pool was still in its making I saw a frog investigating it carefully from one end to the other, obviously gauging its possibilities as a spawning pool. That was four days ago and I imagine she came to the same conclusion that I did: not enough growing vegetation—in fact, none at all, in it. We shall have to wait until next year for that.

And while I was still there, with the water about as thick as the thickest soup, I saw something I had never seen before—a collision between two water-beetles, head-on at full speed. They recoiled, looking very cross, but there was no fight. Visibility was so poor there wasn't even a water-policeman in sight. So there they lay for a while, side by side, discussing the affair.

Later that day my wife and I were standing by the pool, when suddenly, to our amazement, we saw a water-vole, peeping its head round the corner, having come upstream along the little brook. For such an animal—about as big, it seemed, as a half-grown land-rat but much fatter—it must have been quite a tiring walk. These lovely beasts, though rodents, are not in the least like rats. The head of this one was typical vole, so was the short blunt tail, and the body was quite thick.

We stood as still as any garden gnome, which maybe is what he thought we were. In any case, with a sudden bound there he was, standing up like any mouse or vole, forearms in front, bent at elbow and wrist, looking from left to right. Suddenly he turned his head, muttered something which we couldn't hear, and was joined by another.

This one was slightly smaller and somewhat fatter. It could have been the first one's mate. And the pair, we thought, might be looking for slightly deeper water where they could burrow a hole (underwater) slanting upwards, in which to make a nest. They both jumped in, made a quick reconnaisance around the edge, and got out, returning the way they had come.

We very much hope we shall see them back again but fear they will come to the same conclusion the frog did—that the pond is too new, without vegetation and, apart from those few water-boatmen, with no sign of animal life either.

*   *   *

From time to time we notice a neighbour's cat having a snack on our ravens' "table"—the lower paddock where the oxheads are.

I don't mind him picking up a mouthful or so whenever he likes. For he is a pleasant creature and never overdoes his visits by indulging in any kind of greed as the ravens do. Not that he really needs the food, because he is well fed at home.

But the other morning he astonished me. For he had strange company, a small she-cat in dreadful condition, pretty obviously a cat which had recently lost her home, and had not yet learned much about how to survive by living rough.

I was standing beside the nearest head and had stopped a foot or two away. She was eyeing me as if she was afraid, as was probably the case.

I stood still, looking as harmless as I could, and stooped to stroke the purring Tom's head as he rubbed against my leg.

Presently his friend came closer and gave a cautious, half-frightened nip at the oxhead. Her protector stayed by my side and looked calmly at her. This eventually had the desired effect, and she started to eat quite confidently, until she had, at length, had a good meal.

I wondered whether to take them up to the house for a drink of milk, but did not as it would have been a good way of attracting a nice cat away from its home and that would not be a kind thing to do.

As for the starving little she-cat, it was very probable that she would stay with the Tom as his people are very nice with animals and will probably find room for an extra one, and her family when it comes.

Presently they were both finished and after a ceremonial wipe of their noses away they went up the hill to where the Tom's mistress lives and where I suppose the Tom has found a bed for her.

Later, a quick phone call assured us that the little cat had been noticed and was welcome, and food was being provided.

*   *   *

The myxomatosis epidemic of 1953–54 killed off most of our rabbit population, but in some lowland districts their recovery has been marked and they are again plentiful.

In other areas, like up here in the Welsh hills, the increase in rabbit numbers has been meagre in the extreme.

Not only that, but their habits here seem to have changed quite markedly. In the old days they inhabited burrows, either in quite small groups or in communities of several hundred in huge warrens.

Now this is not so. Instinct must have warned them that the gregarious old burrows were where the infection lingered.

Today in these hills there are very few burrows still inhabited by bunnies. The majority of them have become like the American jack-rabbit of Uncle Remus: "Bred'n Bawn en a Briar-Patch, Brer Fox; Bred'n Bawn en a Briar-Patch."

And for some other reason hill bunnies don't breed so numerously as they used to. Before 1953 they bred several times a year and one doe could raise more than a dozen rabbits annually. Today two or three a year is about all.

The other day we were out with the dogs, Teena the shaggy little hunt terrier and Holly the Rottweiler. A few inches of snow had fallen during the night. It was cold, with a pale sun, black cloud banked in the north, and obviously more snow on the way.

Holly was ranging about a hundred yards ahead when suddenly she pointed at a small black blob in the snow which we could identify as a baby rabbit. It didn't seem to be in the least perturbed at the sudden huge arrival but turned to face her, stamping with its hind feet as a rabbit does when it feels that something may be up. Just as well to let Mum know.

And sure enough, Mum arrived at full gallop over the

brow of a little gully a few yards off. At the same moment my wife let fly with a piercing whistle and a yell: "Holly, come!"

That was enough. Holly immediately turned and came flying back, while the two rabbits took their leisurely departure to a nearby bramble patch and disappeared.

*   *   *

Vicky, our young goose, was laying five enormous eggs a week and we felt quite worried about it, wondering whether we'd have to take them into market because we couldn't possibly eat so many, particularly as our eight bantams were laying an average of 40 a week as well.

However, after she had laid ten in her untidy haybay nest she gave up and that was that. My wife took two away and she stayed sitting on eight, though we didn't think she was big enough even for that many.

It was quite a business. To start with, the haybay door broke down, resolving itself into bits and pieces only good for firewood. So every night we have to build a fox-proof barrier of hay bales there and hang some article of unlaundered human clothing on it.

The barrier means that we have to get up early because as soon as dawn appears Albert, Vicky's adoring spouse, who sleeps with the horses and bantams with the bottom half of the door shut, starts yelling his head off as soon as he can see. One or other of us has to get up, let him out and follow him up to the haybay at full speed to open up the hay barrier to let him through.

Then it's a question of their breakfast, after which Albert gives Vicky an affectionate kiss and departs for another breakfast on the bird table. After that he patrols the forecourt, and has a couple of cooling swims in his pool before remembering Vicky again.

Off he dashes to the haybay, reminding me strongly of Charlie Chaplin taking corners at full speed but on the wrong foot.

Once, taking the hairpin corner entry into the haybay, Albert lost his balance completely. I heard him crash to the ground although it was too far round for me to see. However, I heard his language, and also Vicky's derisive reply.

When I got there he was busy preening his ruffled feathers and making excuses. As a matter of fact Vicky sometimes seems quite suspicious of his approaches and pecks him away from her precious eggs.

She also distrusts me being near the eggs. So my wife has to take in her food which she likes to have handed to her while she's sitting.

This is her ninth day on the nest and in all that time she has only been on the pond once. She spent exactly ten minutes off the eggs and in that time was polite to no one. She went for me first. So I came inside. Looking through the window I saw her chase all the bantams off the bird-table while she picked her choice of mixed grain.

She even took exception to a robin and everyone knows what fighting little birds they are; but this one flew straight away with Vicky at his tail.

She was not, thank goodness, quite as fast as the robin. But her huge beak—quite as long and nearly as broad as the entire redbreast—never snapped less than an inch behind its tail, and I wondered if that was intentional on her part.

Soon, though, all was calm on the forecourt and we heard contented clucking emerging from the nest. All was well. She hasn't come down again in the past five days. I do hope she will hatch out at least four or five eggs.

* * *

We saw what was happening while we were still 300 yards away.

A ewe was struggling to produce twins but at the same time trying to hold off a family of four carrion crows that was attacking as mercilessly as only these birds know how.

The two parent birds had already blinded her by pecking at her head, while the two smaller ones, obviously of last summer's breeding, were at the rear end attacking a half-born lamb.

Another lamb lay alongside, feebly moving its legs but utterly helpless. We hurried along as best we could on the steep hillside and as we topped the last little rise our dogs arrived at the scene. With harsh curses, the four birds took off and disappeared over the brow of the hill in seconds.

Holly was licking the prone lamb which the ewe had not had time to clean up.

When we caught up, Holly looked up, then went on with her cleaning, an important job as the lamb was soaking wet from a recent heavy shower.

The ewe had evidently been long in labour and might not have been able to get the second lamb out without help and never would now.

Even as we stood there, she died and so did her last lamb. I picked up the living one and put it in my rabbit pocket to get it back home as fast as possible. And so we left the scene of the pathetic little tragedy.

At home there was little to do except see the new arrival warm and dry, which, after 20 minutes in my rabbit pocket, he was. I was sorry to see that he was a ram because ewe lambs are generally easier to rear than males, and he had obviously got off to a bad start.

However, he had his first drink from a bottle containing evaporated milk with arrowroot, a mixture we have found very effective in the past.

He took this as to the manner born, but I was worried, wondering if he had had time to drink the ewe's first milk, which I believe is important as it contains several medicaments that act as the starter to a lamb's first meals.

The probability is that he never got his first drink anywhere but in our kitchen, which is a pity. However, he got his first bottle down, and kept it down.

After that, Holly gave him another good licking all over. Then we tucked him into a small carton and he was put to sleep in it in front of the fire.

*   *   *

We had been enjoying the view from a mountain several miles to the east of our homestead but now it was time to go home.

We got up from the sun-warmed rock on which we had

been sitting and looked around for Holly. Teena was on the lead as she is not yet entirely sheep-trained.

We didn't have to look far for Holly because she started barking loudly, obviously trying to attract our attention, from the nearby road. After every bark she turned and looked back to a gate across the road with a cattle-grid beside it.

Standing up, we could see that there was no lamb stuck there. So I let Teena slip her lead and down she raced to Holly. They both stood together, looking intently downwards. Obviously there was something underneath the grid—but what?

We trotted down to look, and saw something that gladdened us both—a colossal hedgehog, accompanied by four bright and active little ones with their prickles still soft enough to handle with impunity.

Teena was sitting as good as gold beside the older dog, and I knew why. Last summer she came across her first hedgehog, a huge beast who came regularly for a drop of milk in spring or late autumn.

With a joyous yap the little dog belted forward while the hedgehog just had time to roll itself up and present its prickles to her eagerly inquiring nose. Teena shot back with a wild yell of pain and got into the begging position with both paws up to her nose, yelling continuously.

Teena would never touch another hedgehog, but I was braver. I saw the gap where they had got down under the grid, and put my arm in and pulled them all out.

Presently the sow, followed by her little ones, walked happily off the road and down the hill where they were soon lost in the heavy undergrowth.

And we went home for lunch. But first I inspected the area under the grid, which contained several quite large flat stones, some of them weighing between two and three pounds. Every one had been turned over by that hedgehog to see what lay underneath and I'll bet those little hedge-piggies had a quicker and more varied meal there than ever before.

Even so, I hope they don't go down there again.

* * *

Two things occupy my thoughts as I write: the first is the strange behaviour of a cock chaffinch who has made himself quite notorious among the birds which gather for the food we scatter on the forecourt by his aggressive defence of his own kind.

Nine or ten of the latter, all feminine, are always in attendance as he struts and flutters from one end of the forecourt to the other and back again.

My second thought follows a recent radio programme which suggested that unless we do something about it, there won't be any more breakfast honey on our table.

Why? Because in many parts of England and Wales there is an alarming scarcity of bees. And it is concluded that this is due to the use of pesticides by lowland farmers, vegetable growers and ordinary gardeners.

I wrote about this more than 20 years ago and I received angry letters from vegetable and flower growers. After all, some people have to make their living by the sale of such things.

There are of course insects, millions of them, all over the place and most of them bred and born to damage our fruit, vegetable or corn crops of one sort or another.

There are others that do good, such as bees of all sorts, as well as that curse of the picnic party the wasp, which are essential in the pollination of countless plants.

We do not know how many wasps there are but the bee population is easier to estimate because most bees are domestic, and any good beekeeper knows to within a thousand or so how many rely on him for their sugar when there is no nectar to be had.

We, living on the lower heights of the Welsh mountains, have noticed a scarcity of wasps in the past three years.

Last year the same was true of the bees. Until that broadcast I thought that badgers were responsible because hill-farmers use few pesticides. But I now believe that, even here, pesticides are to blame, because although we are high up in the hills there are valleys a mile away with crop-growing areas 300 feet or even less above sea level where pesticides are used.

Of course, wasps and bees face other dangers too. The

other morning, for example, a very somnolent wasp crawled out of some hidden corner in the morning sun halfway up the window.

I opened the window to let it out, not having noticed our very radical little cock chaffinch which was off the forecourt but right under the window, investigating the daffodils. And as the wasp flew lethargically out, up shot that bird, snapped his beak and two half-wasps fell to the ground. Grabbing up the upper-half, he tweeted to the nearest hen who swooped in on the fatter piece and swallowed it, delighted to be presented with such a tasty snack.

*   *   *

We have had plenty of opportunities of observing the two grey squirrels that have apparently made this cottage and its surroundings their headquarters.

For during almost any day you can see them somewhere about our five acres, either playing or eating.

Now, any country person of 40 years old or more who has a good memory will recall that in the mid-forties there were masses of red squirrels about generally in what I can only call squirrelries, in most if not all our larger parks, particularly those belonging to large estates employing game-keepers.

But by the mid 'fifties a great change had taken place.

The big squirrelries had either vanished or become much smaller.

Today you hardly come across a red squirrel—at least in the district in which I live. While in the middle 'fifties you hardly ever saw a grey squirrel, on whose tail there was a government bounty of half-a-crown.

Since that bounty was abolished, the native red squirrel has vanished almost entirely, while the grey has multiplied enormously.

Some naturalists believe that the grey, a more powerful and aggressive animal, has driven the red out.

But to me it seems more likely that the red squirrels have been practically exterminated by some fell disease similar in effect, though not in outward signs, to myxomatosis in rabbits.

That is what I believe but, having watched our two greys closely, I have begun to wonder about something else as well.

From time to time someone pops up with the claim that he or she has seen an obvious cross-bred specimen, half red and half grey. So far the naturalists have disagreed that they interbreed because it is well-known that at a certain time of the year the grey does to some extent change colour.

This happens in spring when a faintly reddish colour appears on the sides of the animal. At the same time the ears appear to be slightly tufted like those of the red squirrel.

But having had this pair under almost daily observation for nearly three weeks we've noticed that the reddish tint seems to be deepening. And we wonder if we are indeed in the presence of true half-breeds?

*   *   *

However badly some species of our native wild animals have been reduced in numbers during the last 50 years, there is at least one small one which still thrives: the long-tailed fieldmouse.

Quite a number of these live in the thick stone walls of our cottage which, having been built in 1720, has the old-fashioned 22 ins thick walls that nineteenth-century cottages lack.

These walls are honeycombed and the weirdest example of this honeycombing was given to me one night during a blizzard three winters ago.

That night the wind changed to easterly and blew harder, and in the living-room I felt an icy cold draught coming in, but I couldn't decide from where.

Later, having to go out, I reached out to pick up my gumboots from a shelf in a dark corner to the right of the inglenook. But instead of rubber tops my hand plunged into deep, feathery snow which had come in through a mousehole that we were able later to track.

Between entry and exit that tunnel made three turns. Yet that dry snow had followed them all. It was easy to block the holes with cement. And that was that until our last snow-up.

This was also from the east and again, shortly after it started, I was aware of cold but knew not yet whence it came. But when I did, I didn't put my hand down. For I heard a little squeak from the spot.

On the left side of my chair is my old sea-chest, and on the other side of that my wife's chair. Among the clutter of objects on top of that chest lies a torch.

Grabbing it, I shone it downwards to the corner where the original hole had been, to see an open hole partly obscured by what looked like an untidy bird's nest out of which was peeping a small face with two very black eyes.

It was easily recognisable as a long-tailed fieldmouse in her nest, doubtless with a young family. So what to do? Nothing easier.

A little snow was already drifting in and I swept it away with the hearth brush. I got a few bits of wood from my workroom and built a little dam against the hole, leaving just enough room for the mouse to come out. Then I put a saucer down containing milk and a few scraps of cheese with a bit of mutton fat.

And that is the status quo until I search for the outside entry, except that now and again we hear a series of little squeaks in a minor key.

*   *   *

For the last week we have had what we call summer temperatures at this height in the hills; around 34F by night and up to 60F by day.

One winter sign not yet discarded, though, happens to be my long johns; but they never go at least until the may is out and so far there are no signs of it.

The other night I saw a litter of foxes. These little beasts were out, probably for the first time, with their Ma who was obviously taking them for their first little lesson on how to get about quietly with a minimum of noise.

There were four of them, all exactly the same size, all behaving perfectly. When a huge barn owl swept silently over them they instantly vanished under their mother and did not reappear for several seconds. Then they carried on, an obedient little clump of furry bodies a foot or so behind her tail.

When she stopped at one of the fresh oxheads we had put down she started to eat, tearing off a lump of meat which she pushed towards the close line of four little heads, all watching intently.

Cautiously the little ones approached, nosed the meat gently and looked inquiringly at Mum, who courteously stood aside while they started to feed on it.

The vixen carried on with her own meal, now and again chucking a bit to her young. It took them about ten minutes to eat their fill, after which they went as they had come back to their earth, halfway up the opposite hillside.

Some minutes later, when I could no longer see them, I heard a little yelp quickly followed by another, and could easily imagine the scene. Now they were safe in their own bailiwick and could have a little game with Mum, chasing her and being chased in turn, for that is how (and where) they play and learn to be always alert in case of danger.

It will not be long before this little lot are learning some of the sterner lessons of the chase, such as the robbing of local poultry. But for the last two years we've had no minor stock losses from foxes and don't bother about our bantams. For although they nest, feed and roost all over the place, the foxes have learnt that not only do we not shoot foxes but we actually put out food for them and the other predators.

And foxes never raid the place where they get free food. If they need more than is put down for them, they go further afield for it, but obviously knowing that they risk getting shot.

May

Thanks to the late arrival of normal spring weather, there is still hardly any grass on this smallholding's five acres.

Therefore the two donkeys, Rebecca and Naomi, and Patchy, my wife's big skewbald pony, have to be fed on hay and a daily ration of corn.

The other day I went along to feed the patiently waiting three and when I opened the cornbin there, as usual, were two little voles sitting quietly waiting to be let out.

Now, these are wild mice and yet they are tame enough to hop up into the hand of whoever is feeding the beasts and sit there while being lifted out. So I put the hand down and they both hopped into it, one of them sitting straight up and continuing to eat his grain of crushed oat, holding it in his front paws, or little hands if you like, just like a squirrel, only if possible, prettier.

When he had swallowed the last bit, still sitting up, he carefully pulled every whisker individually on each side then, after passing both paws through the fur on his forehead, he got down on all fours and looked up at me as if to say "OK, boss, you can put us down now!"

I did so and they both ambled casually to the nearest mouse-hole and were gone.

This caper started as soon as we installed the galvanised cornbin in the small downstairs granary more than ten years ago. At first we couldn't see how the mice got inside, well knowing that there were no holes in the bottom of the bin and that, except at feeding times, it was topped by a well-fitting iron lid.

Then, one morning my wife, having put out all the feed, returned to shut the bin when she saw a short fat tail vanishing in the oats as the owner of that tail burrowed its way down out of sight. Obviously the little creature had waited for her to turn her back before climbing up the lid, left leaning against the side of the bin.

At first it was a scramble to get the mice out. But they soon got so used to us that on putting a hand down, the mouse or mice—there have been up to three at a time —decided to save us the bother by getting up on to whoever's hand is lowered.

*   *   *

It was a soft, windless morning and through the half-opened window drifted the usual muted sounds of sunrise, with a harsher note from geese and bantams.

All the usual sounds were there plus, a little further off, the occasional lowing of a cow to her calf, the ba-baaing query of a ewe to her lamb, and the replies of their respective little ones.

Yes, all this was usual for a fine spring morning . . . but suddenly I heard a sound I had often heard at this time of year in the past. And, as of yore, it got me out of bed faster than anything else could.

In three minutes I was downstairs and outside with the bantams' feed tin in hand, automatically putting out their breakfast, which on this day two young geese were trying to share.

The other geese I knew were sitting in the haybay, except Albert, who had gone to the pond, for his morning swim, and the noise they were all making, plus the sound of the bantams talking loudly, meant I could no longer hear that softer sound that had got me out of bed . . . that of the mallard.

But I was all eyes, hoping for a sight of the drake or his wife busy making their nest.

And at last I saw them, first the drake with a tuft of winter wool that some ewe had sacrificed on some barbed wire, then his partner close behind, carrying something quite bulky that I could not identify.

From the forecourt I watched as they flew with their

spoils to the nesting-site in the marshier of the two bottom paddocks.

The ducks alighted exactly where they or their kin had last nested three years ago and raised a nice little brood.

Evidently they were not in any kind of a hurry. For after two more leisurely searches for building material they left off, the drake coming up with a small frog which he proceeded to eat, while the duck went for smaller stuff.

Then my wife called me in for breakfast and I left the little newcomers to have theirs in peace.

*　　*　　*

When my wife went out to get water two days ago she was surprised when Holly, our Rottweiler bitch, gave a short bark on emerging from the door, and ran straight up the drive towards the open road.

Naturally my wife followed because both of our dogs are forbidden to go on the road unaccompanied by one of us.

Teena, who is more obedient in some ways, accompanied her. And there at the top they found a lamb, not more than two weeks old, lying in the middle of the drive. She could not get up because one foreleg was held between two stones, each one big enough for her to remain captive.

My wife freed the little thing, a very young ewe, who baaed pitifully as she was carried to the living-room and examined carefully.

There was no visible wound, nor was she in any pain. No bones were broken and there was no undue tenderness anywhere. But when we put her down, she was slightly lame on the foreleg which had been pinned by two heavy boulders.

We came to the conclusion that she had been knocked down by a car that couldn't stop in time. For young lambs are stupid things and often run straight into danger.

The mother had obviously run off as there had been no sign of one anywhere along our lane. We also felt that the lamb had almost certainly been carried to our drive by whoever had knocked her down, anchored safely by two boulders so that we should find her, and driven off.

That too would have been a stupid thing to do, but we know that there are many people living up here who know nothing about sheep.

Anyhow, whoever it was, we were grateful for the thought, and soon that lamb was busy sucking away at a bottle. She took to human beings as to the manner born, and having had her drink lay down in front of the fire and went to sleep.

My wife went out to see if she could locate a ewe looking for a lost lamb. Within half an hour she had returned without having spotted our frantic ewe. So we decided to phone our nearest neighbours who have large flocks.

We were not surprised when the first said he had no speckled-face sheep on his place, his flock consisting solely of the little native all-white sheep, and pedigrees at that. The second was out, doubtless at market. So we called up the third, and found that our little lost one was his.

For this we were thankful because our living-room is small, nearly always containing two human beings and the two dogs. And although we have but little stock nowadays, there is always much to do around the place.

So, after giving her a farewell bottle of milk, she was ready for our neighbour when he arrived, and we said goodbye as he carried her to his car.

She baaed back to us . . . and so they went.

*   *   *

On our walk my wife was ahead on the bank of our local "striver"—she gave it that name because, she says, it's a little stream striving to be a river.

And a river it becomes when it gets to the next, bigger stream. Even in our bottom paddock where it starts, it has a little pool in which we have found bullheads, little fish that like to hide under stones. That shows you how even as a sourcelet, it is striving to be a river.

I hurried up to join my wife and as I got nearer she put finger to lip. I approached as quietly as possible and she whispered that she had seen a kingfisher, actually fishing.

Never having seen a kingfisher catching an awkward-shaped bullhead I doubted it, although this quite ample pool—as big and nearly as deep as our goose-pond—could quite easily contain minnows.

We didn't see a kingfisher again that day. But the next morning was calm and warm with a bright sun. So down to the pool we went quite early, without the dogs. And we didn't have long to wait for we had only just taken up our positions, I with my short-range telescope and my wife with her navy binoculars, when out flashed a bright blue-and-gold small bird from the nest in a hole under the bank, passing in a steep curve around the pool's shoreline. At one place he splashed in with only his beak under water, flashing out again and away back to his hole. Then out came his mate, making exactly the same flight with a quick splash in the middle and back to the hole.

We couldn't see the young, they were obviously feeding because kingfishers nest about a yard inside their hole. But I guessed that they started nesting in that late-March warm spell we had, just as the tree nesters did. And they are now raising a brood which is big enough to keep both parents on the top all day long.

The male stays with his family because in such waters both water-voles and bank-voles abound. Both these species are omnivorous and therefore baby kingfishers need two parents to look after them, so that at least one sharp dagger of a beak is on guard against predators while the other beak is fishing.

*   *   *

After a week without a single drop of rain we have had several showers in the last few days.

But during that dry spell we had drought conditions up here and had to get out water from the village pump.

Which reminds me that Patchy, my wife's gelding, discovered the original well from which this smallholding gets its name—*Pantfynnonlas*, which means the blue well in the dingle.

Tradition has it that it never dries up, but the well that we were told was *the* well has dried up on us nearly every summer since we have been here and when we have a dry spring.

It must have been three years ago that we found out where the proper well was. During a dry summer we noticed that Patchy was never bothered about the water we put out for him and the donkeys. They used nothing else, but Patchy used to come up every morning with his legs muddied up to the elbows.

When we located the spot it was down in the most shaded part of a steeply-sloping paddock. An area of roughly 20 yards by 20 was deep mud and one day Rebecca, our senior donkey and mother of Naomi, tried to follow Patchy.

Patchy had ploughed himself out of two feet of mud, leaving Rebecca to get herself out.

But of course she couldn't, and it wasn't until we heard her bawling away for help that we went down to extricate her.

Then a very old man in his nineties, who had been born in this cottage all that time ago, told us that the muddy patch had been the original well. But to put it back into use the corner would need to be fenced off and the mud patch drained. Then the well would have to be concreted.

My wife went down there not long ago and came up in some excitement. There were, she said, little fish in that well. I couldn't believe it, but she insisted.

And when we got down there, there they were. I dislodged a large flat stone on the bottom and out they came. Now this was a most extraordinary thing, and I can quite believe this is the old, original well.

There must be an underground connection to a larger supply higher up the mountain, and these little fish must have come down in that. And I can quite believe this is the never-failing blue spring down in the dingle.

So this is what we are going to do: fence off that entire corner, even though it will mean carrying enough water for Patchy to drink out of the trough that the donkeys use.

At the same time we shall drain that huge mudbath that he has made around the well. Then on a concrete base, we shall install our little motor and its pump, after which our property will really deserve its old name.

*   *   *

We have had torrents of rain for the past week. No matter. Even if it snows, the sun is now high enough in the heavens to ensure that the cold will not be bitter enough to kill or even endanger the lives of the countless young fledglings and other wild beasties of hillside and upland moor that will see life for the first time in the next couple of months.

Here we have only to go outside our door to hear the supposedly sad cry of the curlew, the pipe of the peewit, plus of course, the mellifluous notes of the countless other smaller birds near the cottage.

It is very noticeable now that most of the birds lingering around the bird-table or the forecourt are males—just as in any pub and for exactly the same reason.

The females we do see are invariably in a hurry to eat as much as they can in the shortest possible time in order to get back home before the eggs cool off or before the fledglings die of starvation

There are a few exceptions. Ravens and carrion crows mate for life and it is fascinating to see how their family life is worked out. Four years ago I stopped shooting these predatory birds because it occurred to me that if we made this smallholding into a bird sanctuary we should logically include predators, if only to reduce their attacks on weakly lambs.

That was the start of what we jokingly call the Field of Golgotha, or the Place of Skulls, because every week we have put down at least two and sometimes three oxheads. Unfortunately Ken, our butcher, always removes the tongues before heaving them into the back of the pick-up. Never mind—there is always plenty left for the birds.

And a significant point is that since we started doing this, there has been a definite local reduction in lamb casualties at lambing time. So it was worth while and now the field and the forecourt bird-table are kept going—and are used —all the year round.

But back to our ravens. Any day now we are expecting to see them appear with their young but in the meantime it is interesting to watch the antics of the parent birds.

Weeks ago the male started tearing off quite large pieces of meat and piling them up. Then the hen would appear, standing by the little pile. Bit by bit he would feed the meat to her and she would gulp it down until the pile was finished and she would fly back to the nest.

Papa would feed for a few minutes and would then start another pile. The wife would arrive, get fed, and go. This would happen three or four times before they would both go, leaving the field open for carrion crows, jackdaws and buzzards.

Occasionally, we get red kites but they are not very brave birds and are easily scared off by magpies, which are very belligerent.

But the more those magpies feed from the skulls, the fewer small birds will be eaten by them. And that is very important—for it is the smaller birds that are most useful to the agriculturalist.

*   *   *

After a local mini-monsoon last week the little stream that feeds our goose-pond was turned into the colour of chocolate.

But by yesterday the water was crystal clear, again revealing the little aquatic creatures that live there.

A trickle of water branches away from the stream to find its way to the pond along a different route and it was here that I stood watching varieties of little beetles messing about in the shallows.

At one point the water was channelled into a cataract about four feet long and a maximum of two inches in width and the little creatures were carefully negotiating this in both directions—tricky navigation for half-inch long insects, though I didn't notice any accidents.

Until, that is, a major incident occurred: a water-rat (more correctly called a water-vole), entered the cataract and proceeded with difficulty to make his way up it.

It appeared to me that the beetles hadn't been properly briefed about this because as this giant forged his way upstream only a few of them managed to swim back out of the way.

I did spot one or two returning in lively fashion to the water as soon as the living juggernaut had squeezed by but others, I suspect, were not so lucky.

Once at the top of the channel the gross intruder hopped on to a flat stone, sat up and started to wash his whiskers, making a very pretty sight as he did so.

With his big blunt, friendly-looking head and very short tail he looked far more vole-like than rat-like and at about eight inches long, not including tail, was obviously one of the parents of the vole family that had made its home in a bank beside the goose-pond.

A couple of minutes sufficed for his toilet before he went on up to the main stream and having lost sight of him I walked back to the goose pond where I amused myself for a half-hour watching his offspring chasing tadpoles.

I did not see any tadpoles being caught and devoured, but that does not mean voles don't eat tadpoles. On the contrary, there were so many tadpoles about that more than likely those little voles had already eaten their fill and were now giving chase for the sheer fun of it.

* * *

Finally, almost too late to call it a spring clean, we have started cleaning and tidying up my workroom, which I share with the beetles, flies (although I don't know what they find to eat there) and the many spiders who live there.

And it was only after we had cleared out over a hundred-weight of old newspapers plus sawdust and other miscellaneous bits and pieces, off the floor that we discovered an enormous stag beetle.

Apparently he had been breakfasting on the sawdust underneath the capacious jaws of my big vice.

However, there was my wife suddenly thrusting her dust-pan under my nose asking what she should do with it. The pan was half-full of sawdust, on top of which (upside-down as might be expected) the gigantic stag beetle was feebly waving his six legs. My immediate impulse was to tell her to chuck it out with its breakfast. But then I hesitated.

For the erstwhile ubiquitous stag beetle lives principally on rotten wood, generally making his home in a dead tree-stump, and it occurred to me that many of the logs that we burn the year round in the living-room are of wood that is well and truly dead and there is usually a pile of their sawdust under the workroom vice.

Also the 22-inch thick cottage walls, built largely of hand-picked small stones, are honeycombed with all sorts of twisty passages, ideal for even the largest stag-beetle.

After putting our beetle (still upside-down) to one side, it didn't take us long to decide to allow him to continue life in such a suitable environment.

When the clean-up was finished I went around our five-acre estate to find a chunk of rotten wood that might be acceptable to our new friend. And eventually found a luscious piece as ripe as it could be without falling to bits.

This I carried carefully back to the workroom, depositing it in a corner where there was a hole big enough for a mouse to get through. My wife then tipped the beetle out of the pan, alongside his new breakfast.

He landed upside-down. So she took a long nail from the bench to turn him over and there we left him.

He stayed there for the next half hour and then he was gone. Doubtless, though, we shall see him again before long.

*   *   *

I was fast asleep in a warm bed. My wife, as I discovered when the drama was all over, was also fast asleep, with her head under the bed-clothes, and therefore half deaf.

Suddenly I was awakened by a commotion going on in the lower paddock where all the oxhead skulls are. I jumped out of bed and looked out of the window. The landscape was lit up by a three-quarter moon in a clear sky. So it was easy to see what was going on.

There were an as yet uncounted number of foxes
gathered in a half-circle around the freshest oxhead which
my wife had put out the night before. And there in the
middle of that semi-circle and almost right up to it was
Albert our gander.

Those foxes were making the nastiest noises a fox can
make at Albert who was making four-foot wing-assisted
jumps up and down and yelling back at them.

Suddenly the biggest fox jumped over the oxhead and
went for Albert. But our brave gander replied with such
quick reflexes that the fox retreated with one eye severely
damaged, if not out altogether.

But there was still the vixen and three half-grown cubs to
contend with, and poor Albert couldn't last much longer. I
grabbed my shotgun and fired over their heads, not mind-
ing if I hit a fox but wanting to aim well clear of our precious
gander.

Then I raced downstairs, clad only with the gun—but
who would care miles up a mountain? Stopping only to
reload the gun and put on a pair of slippers, I ran outside,
yelling bloody murder and firing the shotgun into the air as
I did so and praying that my rescue attempt was not too
late.

It was not. All I could see was four brushes vanishing fast
through the bottom fence—and a triumphant Albert returning at full speed towards myself, warmingly silhouet-
ted against the downstairs lights of the house and still
brandishing the shotgun.

"Are you all right?" I said, and his reply was something
like: "Yes, of course, but no thanks to you for arriving on
the scene far too late."

At that moment from behind the cottage came another
noise that we could both understand without any need for
translation. His wife, Vicky, having heard the commotion,
wanted to be let out from the haybay to see just what was
going on.

Albert and I rushed round the corner and up to the
haybay where, these many weeks, she has been sitting on
her clutch of eggs. I opened the door and she came storm-
ing out. From the noisy conversation they held I under-

stood that he was telling her all about the goings-on and that she was warmingly congratulating him on his bravery.

It struck me as they were acclaiming each other that it might be a good idea to test those eggs in some warm water. And every one floated—the sure sign of infertility.

I believe that those two birds must have read my mind. For it occurred to them that as daylight was crawling slowly over our eastern mountain they might as well go and have their morning bath. They did so in the new bathing pool and since then neither has been near the nest again.

*   *   *

When I was a little boy there was a satisfying predicability about the changing of the seasons.

In December we were skating on the mere, March 21 was the beginning of spring, in February everything was fiercely budding, April showers, which never lasted more than an hour, helped everything to grow and by June 21—the longest day of the year—we were already in the middle of summer.

Since then, nature's calendar seems to have gone haywire. And here we are in the third week of May, with cold rain still falling intermittently and taking its toll of newborn lambs.

Well, weather isn't everything and in the countryside there are compensations, though you have to be up early —as I was a few days ago—to look for them.

One of our dogs had fallen sick and I had been sitting up with her. But at about 4.30 in the morning, I went for a stroll, still in my slippered feet, around the farm.

My first sight of wildlife was in the field where we put oxheads to feed the predatory birds and beasts. A couple of grey squirrels were eagerly attending to the newest pair of oxheads before full daylight, when savage birds such as ravens and magpies would drive them away.

Then, a little farther off, I saw a much darker shape which I identified as a wild polecat, a creature which has become more numerous over the past few years.

Turning left at the bottom of the field I inspected our east boundary fence and was just about to turn back and return to the house when I almost stepped on a huge hedgehog which was being followed by four babies.

I have never quite made out why hedgehogs never stop for my heavy footsteps, but I imagine it is the same reason why so many can be found squashed flat on busy roads. They know that they have prickles, plus the ability to curl up into a ball, and they think that anything, be it cow, car, or man, will try to avoid them.

But this one just went on, followed closely in single file by her babies, up a bank and away down the other side. All but the last little one which turned right, trotted up to my foot, smelt all around it and started to nibble at the toe.

Standing quite still, I looked the little beast over. He had a good coat of well developed prickles which seemed quite sharp, until I bent down to touch them (he seemed to take no notice at all of my attentions) and found them quite soft and bendable.

I presumed him to be about six weeks old, and was glad that he had three brothers or sisters because hedgehogs are a very valuable asset to any country property. But then I noticed that he had already eaten a small hole in the toe of my slipper and was down to my socks.

Lest anything more dire should happen I picked him up and gently chucked him down to where his family had descended the bank. And away he trotted to catch them up, while I walked home with a hole in my slipper which will need all my skill with needle and leather to patch.

*   *   *

I have been keeping a weather record for many years and more than once it has occurred to me that I should also keep a record of the various migrating birds as they come and go.

So, better late than never, I started doing so four days ago by noting the arrival of the two swallows that have started rebuilding the nest—above Patchy the gelding's loosebox —that they used last year. The year before they had nested up in the loft where their parents used to nest before them.

Then one day my wife went up into the loft and found

that nest in pieces on the top of my old sea-chest, complete with two very young and quite helpless small fledglings. The parents were fluttering about in a state of utter disarray, begging us to do something.

We left the little ones on the sea-chest while we glued the nest together. We found an old tin plate and banged a nail hole in the middle, then glued the nest to the plate, putting it into the oven to dry.

When we were satisfied that the glue was hard and that the chicks would not get permanently glued to their nest, we took it back to the loft and, with my feet well apart on the sea-chest so as not to tread on the babies lying there with their mouths wide open yelling for grub, I nailed the plate on to the beam where the nest had been previously.

Then, while the parents buzzed me my wife handed up the chicks and I deposited them in the nest before we discreetly left to give the parents time and peace to get accustomed to the repair.

Within five minutes those birds were out and on the wing, searching high up in the sky for the flying insects on which they live (when they fly high you know that the glass is high too, and there won't be heavy or prolonged rain). Within a few minutes they swooped back to the loft and we followed them in, delighted to see them feeding their infants—comfortably resettled in their old nest and yelling for more—as though nothing had happened.

Until they left for good, the parents always buzzed us as though to say Good Morning. And as soon as the babies learned to fly they did, too. And so it was the first year, when they returned and used the nest that they had been born in, and last year, when, for a change, they nested over the hayrack in Patchy's loosebox. We were always greeted with a friendly buzzing.

This year again they are re-making their nest over the hayrack which, with Patchy on the north side and the donkeys Rebecca and Naomi in the adjoining loosebox, is considerably warmer than the loft.

Things like that are important to birds that regularly migrate, seeking a warm and pleasant clime in which to rear their young. If one horse and two donkeys can make life more pleasant for them, good enough. Certainly, judging by the way we are enthusiastically buzzed whenever we appear on the forecourt, those little birds are well pleased with the arrangement.

* * *

Some weeks ago a solitary jackdaw appeared in the paddock where we put out food for predatory birds and beasts, and he has been around and about ever since.

Until yesterday I regarded him as a confirmed loner. For he always kept very much to himself and never encroached on any other bird's target.

But yesterday morning as I watched from the house, he found something in the paddock that delighted him—the top of a tin cut off by one of those patent openers.

How that had got down there I do not know; possibly it had been discarded by a predatory and jewellery-loving magpie, too civilised to fall permanently for such a common thing.

However, there was the jackdaw blissfully in possession of this beautiful piece when suddenly a young and obviously female jackdaw coquettishly approached him and started examining his prize with great interest, albeit from a foot or two away.

At first he took no notice but busied himself with another scrap of nearby garbage for a few minutes, as if intent on eating it himself. But then he shyly pushed the morsel towards the newcomer, who thereupon changed her tactics and immediately went right up to the shiny piece to examine it at close quarters. Whereupon he hopped up to her side and stayed there.

Then the phone went, and it was someone who would not believe he had a wrong number but rang me three more times in quick succession to say he wanted to speak to someone I had never heard of. And by the time I got back to the window there was no sign of the birds.

I even went down to the paddock to see if they had left their shiny piece of tin. But there was no sign of it.

It was highly probable that a romance had started, but I

wondered if they had joined up with the little hen's larger bunch a few miles away or whether they would remain a lonely couple. Quite probably, I thought, the latter.

I hope so because jackdaws, always one of my favourite birds, are cheerful, neat and tidy little things.

When I was very small we had a tame one which had a cage in a front window but which was free to go all over the house, all round the garden and anywhere else though it never ventured far.

It was a fluent speaker and once caused trouble in the house for a cousin of mine who attempted, only too successfully, to teach it just like sailors used to teach their parrots—to speak the worst of bad language!

June

The other day my wife was down at the bottom end of our well paddock when Holly and Teena kicked up an extremely urgent alarm and disappeared into the middle of an extensive blackberry thicket.

At the same moment, out of the top end dashed two quarter-grown foxcubs streaking like hell and yelling for Mama to come and save them.

By the time our two dogs had sorted themselves out of that very thick thicket, the cubs were just vanishing through the gate halfway up the paddock. But no matter. They both knew what they were after and both knew how to run on scent alone. By the time my wife got to the gate, there were the two dogs, both digging like mad. We called them off and returned to the house, returning with a rake after shutting the dogs in, and blotting all sign of dogs' feet on the smooth earth.

Much later that day we went there just before sunset, finding on the raked surface the marks of one adult which had come just far enough to stick his or her head out, sniff a few times, and wait until all was quiet before coming out.

We don't mind them because the generally accepted old wives' tale is true in most cases. And that is that a fox who lives on any farm does his hunting on other people's farms, as long as he is not molested by his own farmer—in which case he moves.

So good luck to them, and I may have more to tell about them as they grow up.

* * *

It was a perfect day. At 9 a.m. there was a cloudless sky, a warm sun still hanging low and a surface temperature of 65F.

We were walking along a narrow ride in the forest, my wife, myself, Holly the Rottweiler bitch and Teena, the short rough-haired hunt terrier of indeterminate origin we got from a dogs' home.

That day Teena and Holly were 50 yards ahead of us, busily sniffing about in hope of putting up a rabbit, hare or perhaps a grouse, partridge or pheasant. We don't stop the dogs doing this as they have never been known to catch —or even look like catching—any of the aforementioned fauna.

Suddenly Teena pointed and gave a sharp yap. Immediately, Holly bounced into the low brush surrounding some young conifers and out, like a bat out of hell, shot a large fox going away from us with something in its mouth.

Both dogs were close behind it but my wife was ready with her whistle and blew several short blasts. Teena was the first to come galloping back, but to our surprise, not to us.

She stopped dead and vanished into the brush from which the fox had appeared. A few seconds later her head poked out and she barked a peremptory note at us, standing there waiting.

We hurried over and a quick glance revealed the whole story. Around what remained of a pheasant's nest were bloodstained feathers and three smashed eggs.

The fox had obviously killed the hen and in the struggle some eggs had been broken. Had we not appeared the killer would have eaten the rest of the eggs and taken the bird home to its young family, which by now would be six or seven weeks old, lively and ravenous. Well, that fox had got away with a meal for the family. As for us, the dogs had found us a clutch of pheasant eggs for a bantam to sit and hatch. They were still warm and I pocketed them before we hurried off home, fortunately only a little over a mile away, before they could cool off.

And we made it too. Roly, the bantam, had only started sitting earlier that morning. So we removed her eggs to eat as we have more than enough bantams to keep us in eggs all the year round.

And if she hatches out the pheasant's eggs, we will raise them and, when they are old enough, turn them loose near their mother's old nest in the forest.

* * *

The other day we decided to take a look at the granary loft under the roof at the north end of the cottage.

This used to be a reserve haybay, with two doors where bales of hay could be winched up. One of these doors remains but the other, facing the forecourt, was blocked up about 100 years ago.

As I was getting out the ladder I remarked to my wife that we haven't seen many sparrows about this year, except the hedge accentors which are not really sparrows at all. They are quite useful little birds, mainly living on the more harmful insects.

But what we discovered in the loft was more exciting than any sparrow: a family of jackdaws. And from the noise they were making, quite a raucous little lot, consisting of the two parents and three to five chicks.

They were nesting by the end of the north roof beam where they had plenty of room for a not very tidy nest.

The cock bird was inclined to be aggressive, but kept his distance as he didn't know which one of us to attack.

However, we were in no real danger at all as we are quite well known to all jackdaws hereabouts as the proprietors of the bird-tables which quite a flock of them help themselves to every winter, and in summer, too, for as long as they want to avail themselves.

But this year, since summer started, I hadn't seen them.

In any case, we have this family now and I very much hope to keep them well fed and happy.

This shouldn't be too difficult because yesterday, just after lunch, a noise outside alerted the dogs who both jumped to the window and started giving tongue.

I jumped up and there outside, tapping on the window in a manner that brooked no delay, was the hen bird of the new family. So I immediately put out some meat. By the time I had done that the cock bird was there too, and we were kept entertained by them both for the next 20 minutes.

So there we are; we have a new little family to look after and I very much hope to keep them.

*   *   *

We have a hare in the house and she is getting along nicely in my workroom where cats, dogs and donkeys are not allowed. Her left hind leg is off at the joint, the upper part exposed to the open air, but nice and clean.

The part above the amputation is sprayed daily with a nauseating preparation nowadays called Bitter Apple, although when I was a kid with a tendency to bite my nails in times of stress, they used to anoint my fingers with bitter aloes which is exactly the same.

This hare took one bite at what was left of her leg—and one only. Now she leaves it strictly alone.

What happened was this. We had been to town on market day to do our shopping which included three oxheads (our butcher gives them to us free because he, too, is a member of the Royal Society for the Protection of Birds) for the weekly supply of food for the ravens, carrion crows, magpies, not to mention one jaybird which, if the meat supply looks like running out, knocks angrily on the living-room window, buzzards and the occasional red kite.

We were driving about halfway back up the mountain when we spotted this hare in the middle of the road lying on its side. We stopped, my wife got out, picked it up and brought it back, greatly to the fascination of our Rottweiler bitch who always comes with us, as she is very well-behaved in the Land-Rover.

That hare had been bounced about a bit because she lay calm in my wife's lap all the way home.

Ten minutes after arriving home, her leg had been taken care of and instead of being consigned to the fate of jugged hare (she would have lasted us for half a week) she was quite comfortable in a carton in my room with half a lettuce to nibble.

And now, four days later, she is happily learning to get about on three legs. By the middle of next week we will be able to let her go in a field where we found her.

Looking after such an animal is not sentiment at all. It is just a question of attempting to halt the decline in wildlife, which, when I was a boy, was bountiful. That young doe, which would have died, will now live to produce her kind.

* * *

We have been slightly re-arranging our fencing due to having found Patchy, my wife's skewbald gelding, up to his stomach in the goose-pool and having a glorious time splashing about and showing off outrageously.

Patchy is very much of a show-off provided there is an audience. Whenever we ride into town, for example, we pass a superstore which has five or six huge windows, extending for a good 30 yards.

Consequently, when we ride by Patchy gets a superb view of himself with his owner perched on top like a sparrow, and he immediately starts behaving like a show-horse in a dressage event.

A few paces before he can see his reflection in the first window he starts loudly pawing the road with his shining shoes and well-blacked hooves. He snorts loudly and, on a cold day, sends puffs of steam out of his flaring red nostrils.

Passers-by stop passing by, which the horse well knows will happen. Proudly he nods his head at them and then goes into the first part of his routine. Though he has never really been taught to do it, he can go sideways very gracefully, five or six paces to the right to get a bit nearer the windows, then two or three back again; now right again and then into an absurd slow trot, bringing all his legs up high one after another.

After the last window he resumes his normal six miles per hour jog and on we go, to the applause of the audience.

So there, now, was Patchy in the middle of the goose-pond. He already had an audience of two donkeys (who seemed to be in two minds about joining him) and the geese sitting along the top of the bank. By the time we got him out and into his loosebox with a dipper of corn, we had made up our minds. We'd make a fence from the main entry-gate to the back of the house, which would cut off entry to the pond from the forecourt.

We would have more fencing behind the house, a small gateway between the garden wall and west paddock and the pond and the Old Garden plus the whole of the west paddock for two goats, the gander, geese and goslings.

Patchy could go without a bathing pool. After all, never before had we known him to go swimming voluntarily. Indeed, he never liked even small and innocent streams, except for drinking purposes.

Indeed, the first time my wife tried to take him over a shallow water jump he tried to turn back in mid-air, landing her in the water.

*   *   *

We went in for poultry the year after we bought this little place, starting off with three bantams, a Rhode Island cockerel and two pullets of mixed breed.

Then we acquired six bantam chicks from a friend and all the hens, just ordinary farmyard biddies that they were, turned out to be massive layers, scattering eggs all over the place.

They also produced small clutches of from one to four chicks which they raised, and these offspring eventually did the same, leaving us to do very little apart from feeding them well. So that now we have one cockerel, seven hens and three clutches totalling eight chicks all under one week old.

I readily agree to deplorable husbandry, but this haphazard system seems to work and although we only produce three or four small clutches annually, they all turn out well and every time my wife sallies forth in the laying season she comes back with at least a week's supply of eggs.

But there's a wee fly in the ointment regarding breakfast time on the forecourt.

The culprit is Mrs H, an original member of the second bunch who has certain very prickly characteristics, such as the belief that the best defence is all-out attack, no matter what the size of your opponent, be it my wife's horse Patchy, who weights a good 1,200 lb, down to Holly the Rottweiler, and Teena the hunt terrier.

Patchy, who wouldn't hurt a fly, takes no notice whatsoever, but both dogs stand in mortal fear of her, and of her chicks as well, although they appear to be normally mannered little things and take no notice.

She has mellowed a little over the years, except when as now she has chicks. The poor dogs are afraid to put their noses out of the door if she is anywhere on the forecourt, and unfortunately in this recent bad weather she has taken to sitting on the doorstep with her three chicks comfortably warm and dry underneath her.

There she was yesterday, when for the first time she went for my wife. The bantam attacked her at full gallop just as she was coming out of the living-room with another can of chicken corn. My wife went flying back into the room, ending up in the fireplace on top of poor little Teena, who came off very much third best, while Holly vanished into the kitchen with the cats.

Within seconds the living-room was full of biddies mopping up the spilled corn, and Mrs H, satisfied that the enemy was vanquished, gathered up her babies and joined in.

*   *   *

The other day was a real midsummer scorcher. The sun came blazing into our bedroom at the crack of dawn and soon had me awake and Holly the Rottweiler stirring from her sheepskin rug under the window.

As I started to dress she looked round at me with a shy grin, knowing that she and Teena would be let out for an early run.

While they were enjoying themselves in the west paddock, I went to have a look at the goose-pond. Sure enough, like most of our mountain streams, the one that feeds it had shrunk as a result of this spell of hot days, but it was still at least two and a half feet deep in the middle. True, it was a bit dirty but it was still clear enough for me to see half a dozen water-boatmen beetles oaring themselves about with their long paddle-shaped hind legs. I knew that if they were there, so would be all the other summer denizens of that little pool.

Then, out of the long grass on top of the bank and on to the bare, steep slope down to the water's edge appeared a mole. Spreading his wide, spade-shaped front legs apart and walking slowly with his hind legs, he more or less slid down to the water's edge, dipped in his muzzle and began to drink.

He hadn't taken more than four or five swallows when another obviously thirsty mole appeared at the top of the bank and was halfway down before the first one saw, smelt or heard him.

And moles are naturally antagonistic. They live in the dark and when they emerge into the sunlight all they ever seem to want to do is fight.

The first mole whipped round, shot up the bank in a flash and next moment they were in a fighting clinch with their front legs. A second later they rolled down the slope and hit the water with a splash. Once more apart and out of the water, they waded into each other with sweeping hay-makers.

The smaller one of the two then landed a right uppercut to the jaw and the other backed up the slope into the long grass while his opponent descended in leisurely manner to the pool and had his drink.

*　　*　　*

Bats are our only surviving backboned animals capable of true flight.

Unlike birds, bats have four feet, connected to one another by their wings. They have fur and in their mouse-like mouths are sharp little teeth.

They also have a built-in radar system far better than anything that so-called higher-ranking mammal man has yet been able to design.

This system enables a bat to fly in a pitch-dark room full

of long-haired women without ever getting tangled up in
their hair. And what if you were to take all those frightened
(but totally untangled) women out of that room, turning
two fat moths loose there instead?

If you open the door ten minutes later the bat will quite
probably fly out and away to his normal day-time dormi-
tory, squeaking his thanks to you as he goes. On the floor, if
you look closely, you will find two perfect sets of moth-
wings. The moths, remember, were released to fly about as
the bat was. Yet in total darkness he was able to track them
down like a Sidewinder missile.

Dr Maurice Burton says in a book on bats which he
revised some 30 years ago that we have 12 distinct kinds of
bat in Britain. That long *ago* he was right.

Today, after the 1953–4 epidemic of myxomatosis that
killed off our rabbit population and therefore changed our
ecology entirely, there are no longer so many. When we
lived up a mountain in Montgomeryshire I wrote about the
Valley of the Bats. Then there were thousands of huge bats
up there. You could walk up that valley and count them on
a sunny day hanging from the trees like grapes.

Today there isn't one left. The stoats and polecats learnt
to climb trees when there were no rabbits left—and that
was the end of them.

I was very happy the other night when my wife came in
after taking the dogs out for their last pre-bedtime walk.
She said that there were pipistrelles all over the place. So
out I rushed.

They are the tiniest bats of the 12 types that we used to
have, and there they were, a dozen or more, flying round
the bright outside light, making breakfast, tea, dinner and
supper out of the countless moths and small flies buzzing
around that globe.

We have seen them in increasing numbers since early
April, so it would appear that they at least have survived
the raids of stoat, weasel and polecat. Long may they
continue to do so, I thought, as I watched them feed until
they left with stomachs bulging.

*   *   *

It was a chilly but dry morning and we took the dogs for a good hour's run so that they would be obedient and quiet when we arrived at our destination.

This was the nesting site of our kingfishers. We wanted to see if they had successfully raised the brood they had been feeding when we had watched them in May. We had not returned until now for fear of disturbing them.

Most of the wildlife we encounter seems to be more or less accustomed to their environment being shared by a couple of human beings and our various dogs, which have been trained from an early age, never to chase anything.

After following the fast-flowing little stream for about a mile we eventually arrived upwind of the pool where we had seen the birds. It is a wide, deep pool, sometimes as still as a mill pond, and, sometimes, in the winter after the snow has melted or after heavy rain, a churning cauldron.

That day it was very full but reasonably quiet. We settled down among the bracken in a small copse of young ash to wait, with a well-earned biscuit apiece for the dogs and sandwiches for ourselves.

Half an hour later we had still not seen any sign of our kingfishers, the dogs were getting restive and I was feeling decidedly chilly.

We were just thinking we might as well go home when Holly the Rottweiler suddenly stiffened. A quick signal from my wife kept her down, but the cause of the excitement was not the kingfishers.

Instead, out of the reeds along the bank appeared a moorhen. He circumnavigated the pool twice, rhythmically jerking his head in the characteristic way of the moorhen.

Obviously deciding it was safe, he gave a couple of "chirricks" and out of the reeds came his wife and four chicks. More squawks from both parent birds brought out three more babies.

We had seen mallard and the odd heron on this pool before but never moorhens and we do wonder where this pair came from and what they are doing up here in the hills.

Anyway, we are very glad to see them because the little family will be safe from the major predator on the lowland lakes and rivers, the pike, which takes its toll of young water birds.

We watched the moorhens for a few more minutes and then, with the dogs at heel, we slunk away quietly so as not to alarm them. Only when we were well up the hill did we let the dogs go to chase each other about until we arrived home.

But in a few days we will return, this time in the evening when there may be more chance of spotting our king-fishers.

*   *   *

A few days ago I walked out to meet my wife who was returning on Patchy the pony after exercising the two dogs in the hills.

We had seen each other from a mile apart, she on one hilltop, I on another. We waved and I sat down for a breather on a convenient and nicely warmed rock amid the heather.

She would obviously arrive in about ten minutes, but in the meantime my eye had spotted a slowly advancing bird.

It was a kestrel, a high-flier which can remain hovering over the same spot for minutes with almost no wing movement before descending like a rocket on its prey—generally a vole or field mouse.

As I was sitting on a rock in the middle of almost face-high heather and, as always, wearing inconspicuous clothes, I was surprised when this one stopped dead almost directly over me.

Had I been spotted? Kestrels have amazing eyesight, but there he or she was, absolutely stationary without a single wingbeat in a gentle breeze.

Then I caught sight of movement about five yards away on another rock just slightly above the heather-line. Up it was climbing a vole, one of those attractive little fat-bodied, short-tailed, blunt-headed huge-eyed little mice that I've always loved because they are so beautiful and so easily tamed.

Was this little beauty going to make a lunch for a kestrel?

Over my dead body. I jumped to my feet with a hoarse roar and threw my hat up at the bird.

The kestrel swerved violently and was off at full speed but only to get another fright. For dead ahead of it was my wife advancing at a gallop with two wildly bouncing dogs.

The dogs had been bouncing to see what they were chasing, as they were below the heather-line. Then my wife arrived, holding on to the saddle to keep herself from falling off with laughter. The vole had vanished.

*   *   *

One branch of my family consists of what were called, less than 100 years ago, yeomen farmers. Another branch was pure horse romany about which I shall write in my autobiography if I ever get round to writing it . . .

Meanwhile, I assure you that I am just an old countryman who can read and write but whose knowledge of the countryside is about 90 per cent gained from observation and the passed on wisdom of the long-gone, like old Kayleg Propert, our scythe man, when I was a small boy.

Kayleg was a peasant. I use the word not in the sense of the bare-footed beggar running alongside a coach begging for alms, as he did in Thackeray's day, but in the knowledge that it comes from the Latin—or French and Spanish words —for Man of the Country, which is just what I am: *un paisano*, a man of the country.

It is this lack of book learning on the countryside that led me the other day to look up an old book on voles and other members of the so-called *muridae* family.

A few weeks ago, soon after we built our new goose-pond, I noticed two water voles inspecting it.

Now, during the day, when the geese have messed up the pond by cleaning themselves in it, one can see nothing there except a few leaves and goose feathers floating about on top. Plus a dozen or so little pond-skimmers rushing about on the surface.

Later, when it has cleared, one also sees the bigger water-boatmen displaying their skill a few inches below the surface. And if you go out a few minutes after dusk or after dawn, you may be lucky to see one or two water voles swimming about in it.

It is not surprising that they have made it their base because the nearest other pool in which they can swim is at least half a mile downstream and when they get there they are only 200 yards from the main stream.

It seems to us, therefore, that wherever they have their nest, our pool is where they will teach their offspring to swim. And I hope this is so because I would love to test out what I read in that old book that, like other short-tailed and bank voles, water voles are just as easily tamed. I've long known that land voles are easy to tame, but I've never had a water vole from babyhood and this will be my chance.

Meanwhile, we have had a bantam hen sitting on six duck eggs and the other day she hatched five ducklings. So even if we don't see or hear much more about the water voles, there will soon be something to write about: ducklings giving their mother a heart attack by learning to swim.

*   *   *

We had been driving along a piece of our mountain road that I thought I knew like the back of my hand when disaster struck.

The culprits had come blinding around quite a sharp corner in a van carrying small children, with a spade sticking out of one window and a shrimping-net out of the other.

They passed us waving gaily and giving a couple of toots on their horn as they vanished round the corner.

To avoid them I had to move sharply to our left—just too far as it happened. For our Mini slid down into the ditch and became firmly stuck, the left wheels having nothing to bite on except water and soft mud.

Anyway, we had a brushing-hook in the car and I was using this to clear away the lush-growing weeds from around the wheels when, just by the front one, a fieldmouse appeared, accompanied by three youngsters.

They were remarkably tame and didn't get out of our way at all. In fact they hung about as though trying to tell us something and it was pretty obvious what; that one of their company was missing and could we help?

We were just wondering how when a tractor made itself heard, eventually rumbling to a stop beside us. The driver, a boy who looked about ten or so, opened the proceedings by announcing: "I see you've found our Dotty and her babies."

He went on to explain that he had been feeding the little family regularly since coming across them one day and they had taken to waiting for him at the very spot where our car had come to grief.

"But wait . . . one of the babies is missing," he said.

At that moment, though, the fourth baby appeared with nothing worse than a bruised tail, and that only at the tip where a wheel must have gone over it.

The tractor lad examined the little creature carefully before putting him in his jacket pocket, where he was shortly joined by the rest of his family.

After the tractor pulled us on to the road again the cheerful driver told us that after our departure he would release the mice and give them their daily meal of bread and milk.

So, with loud farewells, our thanks and a chocolate bar we left him there and continued on our way.

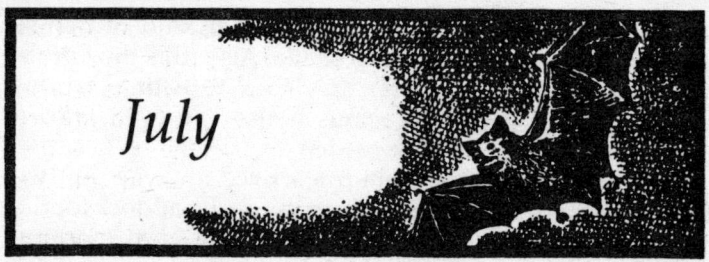

July

The two little foxes and their mama who recently moved into an old rabbit-hole near our cottage are still there and occasionally we see them, either late at night or early in the morning, playing around quite happily.

So far they have taken no chickens, nor molested our geese, and we hope they continue to behave.

Early the other morning I looked out of a window towards the paddock, and there were two cubs in the middle of it, happily playing with the vixen.

Sneaking out of the house, I had a beautiful view of them as they fiercely attacked their mama, only to get gently batted over their little heads in return.

They were having a lesson in self-protection, and having a great time, too. They were not bothering about keeping quiet either, making savage little growls continuously.

Then I saw something that really fascinated me. . . . About 50 yards from the three foxes several rabbits were at play.

There were three young ones busy nibbling away at the fresh dew-scattered grass while sitting straight up and looking in my direction was the doe and I don't believe she could see the foxes because there was a thick hedge on a low bank between them.

But rabbits have very keen hearing, and even I, about as far away from the foxes as the doe, could hear the growls and snarls of the cubs. Yet she gave no sign, though she was obviously on the alert, and her three little bunnies went on busily filling their bellies.

Now, rabbits used to provide more than 70 per cent of a fox's food until myxomatosis swept 99 per cent of them into oblivion. So foxes had to learn to eat other things—

including frogs and voles and any other kind of mouse available; plus rats, slugs, and snails. Also (this they probably learned from badgers) they took to eating various kinds of roots. At our previous house I've even known them eat parsnips from the garden.

The night after the present trio arrived my wife put two fresh oxheads in the usual place in the skull paddock for the crows, bigger birds, badgers and so forth. Next morning one was missing and I found it just outside the new earth, half hidden under a bush.

So from there on we have been putting two heads a week there. If they are eating rabbits as well (and there are far more around this year than I have seen since the epidemic) they are at least leaving those on our land alone.

As I continued watching, one of the cubs must have bitten the vixen too hard. For suddenly she gave a sharp yelp of pain and immediately the big doe stamped violently with her hind legs. The baby rabbits bolted at full speed for their thicket, closely followed by mama. And the foxes went on playing.

*   *   *

The big day had arrived—the day Holly our Rottweiler was going to her second dog show—and we were up at 5 a.m.

Holly had been bathed the previous night and shone like black gold. She knew something was up and was excited; a short walk (at six in the morning!). Something was definitely up and she knew that she was the target.

At her first show she had won one second prize and two thirds. Now we hoped she would do even better.

We set off at 7 a.m. driving slowly because Holly, like her Auntie Meg before her, can suffer from car-sickness and nobody taking a dog to a show wants that.

My wife is the show-ring handler. So there was I sitting in the circle of eager watchers, carrying a wooden spoon in one pocket in case Holly should win nothing.

In such cases my wife sends the dog over to me, I present her with the wooden spoon, she takes it back and gives it to the judge, who hands it back to her with applause from the audience. But in this case it wasn't needed.

She sat on the judge's feet; she looked up at him and grinned her ghastly grin, even rubbed her head on his knee. He remarked to my wife that she really had something there, and that once Holly got a bit more accustomed to the ring she would go a very long way. Actually, when we counted up the awards, we wondered just how far you can go at Crufts, because in this one relatively small show alone she had three Firsts, one Second, three Thirds and best of all, the grand green and purple rosette for Best of Breed. Eight prizes in all!

On arrival home there were other things to be done before having a celebration drink. Such as releasing our five new ducklings and their foster-mum, Lady, a very fussy bantam who is very energetic.

Those ducklings made a galloping beeline for the goose-mere in the Old Garden and were soon disporting themselves on it, to the disgust of the water-boatmen and pond-skimmers that had previously been there without interference.

And there was a very agitated Lady, making an exhibition of herself by rushing up and down on the nearest shore-line emitting enough noise for a dozen bantams. And of course, Holly, full of prizewinning glory, had to add her little bit to the confusion. She took a running jump and landed with a great splash in the middle of the pool.

With a dreadful screech Lady slid off her perch on a mound of clay and splashed in as the ducklings rocked up and down quite unperturbed, like tiny landing-craft under heavy air-attack.

"Come out, you hooligan!" I yelled to Holly, and my wife gave a squeal of delight. I asked what was the matter as the turmoil on the pool subsided.

"That's just what we wanted," she replied, "Holly isn't a long enough name. Now we can enter her in all shows as Holly O'Hooligan and she'll be a certain prizewinner."

But pride goeth before a fall. Only last week Miss Holly O'Hooligan entered her third show and naturally this time I had not taken a wooden spoon in my pocket, so sure was I that she would triumph again.

But she came nowhere in every class. And only later did

we learn that the judge had never seen a Rottweiler and had mistaken Holly for a mis-begotten cross between a great Dane and a pug-dog.

At least I've learnt my lesson: not to leave that lucky wooden spoon at home again!

* * *

The buzzard was flying low—as they often do when returning home—across the moorland. In his beak he had a large fieldmouse or young rat, obviously taking it to his nest to feed his young.

I was out walking, going to meet my wife who was exercising the dogs on a mountain top about a mile from our cottage.

The buzzard approached when I was still on the mountain road, seven or eight feet wide, on which holiday motorists unaccustomed to such narrow highways often get into trouble.

I was carrying no gun but when the bird was only 50 yards away from me he suddenly decided I could be dangerous and swerved violently up and away, hitting the single telephone wire and falling like a stone on to the middle of the hard road, head first. And there he lay, not moving, his eyes closed.

He was obviously knocked out, not by contact with the wire but by hitting the road with the flat of his head. There was no knowing whether he was concussed or not. If so it might take a long time for him to recover.

I could have easily taken him home where we could have looked after him but there was a snag: I thought of his own home with a mother and several chicks all waiting for his return with lunch, the chicks all looking skyward with wide-open beaks yelling blue murder.

I walked a few yards away, took a pinch of snuff and settled down behind a tree to think beautiful thoughts as I always do when waiting for inspiration, not forgetting to keep part of my mind on the matter in hand.

After a few minutes I heard a scuffling noise on the road out of sight. I peeped round the tree trunk. There was my buzzard, staggering about in a circle around his prey—

which I now saw was a half-grown rat. Good for him, I thought, wishing I could give him half an aspirin.

Five minutes later he picked up the rat, shaking it violently to make sure it was dead (in all the confusion he probably wasn't quite sure what had happened).

Then, as his memory returned, he knew he must avoid that wire. So he went to the edge of the lane, clumsily but successfully hopped over the narrow ditch, scrambled up the bank and laboriously took off.

For the first 100 yards or so his steering wasn't too good. But it soon improved and after that he was on course for home, family and a good lunch. And I went on to meet my wife and the dogs, and to tell my tale.

* * *

Badgers are highly intelligent creatures, able to think their way through quite complicated manoeuvres.

Many years ago I discovered a bees' nest in an old tree in a forest, having first spotted isolated bees, all flying in the same direction. After following bee after bee, each one flying along exactly the same line, I came to the tree which they entered by a hole about 12 ft up.

I got near enough to it to examine another, much larger hole in the trunk at ground level. Outside it there was a heap, not of earth but of rotten wood from inside the tree, with a few scraps of honeycomb.

My reasoning was that a badger had spotted the nest, by following the bees just like I had. On coming to the tree he had worked out that the entry hole was too high for a badger to reach by climbing up the trunk, but the tree was obviously hollow. Would it be worthwhile making a hole at ground level and climbing up inside?

The result was obvious to me. He had reasoned aright, and been well rewarded.

I was reminded of all this a few days ago when we were exercising our dogs in a forest half a day's car ride from here.

Suddenly the dogs stopped at a tree not far off, making the sort of noise that always indicates something of great interest, and would we please come along and tell them what it was?

There was a stiff breeze blowing and unfortunately we happened to be down-wind of that tree. For the dogs soon found out what the point of interest was, and came yelping to us for help, followed by a small bunch of infuriated bees.

Telling my wife to grab a double handful of bracken I did likewise and off we all dashed into the wind—the sensible course because bees are slow flyers—passing within 20 yards of the tree in which the bees had made their nest, wildly swiping all around our heads and necks until we were free of them.

Then we got to a small pool and both dogs jumped in to get rid of the last bee. We had come off better, my wife getting stung once, myself only once.

But as we passed that tree I had seen that, once again, there was a huge hole at the roots with a lot of debris all around it, a mixture of rotten timber scraps of honeycomb and suchlike. Obviously a badger family had been enjoying a feast of precious honey.

* * *

One sunny day last week I was sitting on a rock, properly clad to enjoy the beauties of nature. My shirt was a soft green and so were my trousers.

And I was virtually invisible to bird or beast at any range over five or ten yards.

To prove it, a large grass snake appeared on the flat top of a nearby rock. The fact that the rock was protected from the hot rays of the sun by a large bush of broom in full yellow flower made me wonder why the snake, which was at least three feet long, had chosen it.

I would have thought it would have preferred something a little warmer . . . until I noticed something else. The snake had an untidy thickening behind the eyes. Then it started to rub one side of the jaw, then the other, on the rock. And the untidiness slipped slightly back.

The snake was in the process of changing its skin and I was being privileged to witness the process as long as I kept perfectly still. Which I did, since I was anxious to see how long it took.

Little by little, perhaps half an inch at a time, the snake

wriggled out of the old skin with short, sinuous jerks, so that it peeled inside out.

After 15 or 20 minutes there was only about an inch and a half left of the end of the tail. With a triumphant sweep of that tail the snake flung off the last of its old coat, which flew towards me, landing halfway between us. I got up and reached down for it while the snake turned its head and looked at me with crystal-clear eyes. Without any undue hurry it turned and slid away and that was the last I saw of it in its gleaming new coat.

Holding up the old skin to the light I looked through the "spectacles", the membranes that covered the eyes, and could see the broom flowers as clearly as through glass.

So I pocketed the skin to show the "spectacles" to my wife and wended my easy way home.

* * *

For the last week our temperatures have climbed past 80 every day, and haven't fallen below 68 at night, which is why we are sleeping with windows and doors wide open.

Now if a light is turned on while the window is left open we usually get a few moths indoors—big light-coloured ones that normally congregate around the outside light when that is on. There are also often quite a lot of bats about because those same moths provide them with a cheap and easy meal.

The other night my wife and I were awakened by alarming noises from Holly the Rottweiler, who sleeps in our bedroom on her luxurious lambswool rug unless it is too hot, when she lies flat on the floorboards panting and puffing.

As my wife switched on the night-lamp I leapt out of bed and dashed down the stairs after Holly to open the front door.

I switched on the outside light to see how she was getting on in the hunt for whatever had alarmed her. Very nicely, thank you—just attending to an urgent call of nature.

There came a shriek from my wife. I leapt back upstairs to find her in the altogether outside the bedroom, with the door firmly closed.

"An enormous moth flew in and immediately attacked me!"

"Nonsense," I soothed in my best bedside manner. "Moths don't attack people. It was attacking the lamp, as they always do. So what?"

"Well," she replied, "one of those little pipistrelles shot in after it, but I got out here in case one or the other got in my hair."

I opened the door. There was the bat in mid-flight with a colossal moth in its mouth, and when we appeared with Holly between us it made a batline for the window and was gone. I expect it made for its roosting-place in the granary over the looseboxes, there to eat its supper undisturbed.

I looked at the clock: 3.30 a.m. So we turned out our lamp and got back into bed.

*   *   *

It was my wife who discovered our new squirrel family.

There was a skinny grey mother with four babies in a makeshift dustbowl behind the upper granary door.

And as it is some years since I clambered up into this bastion of our cottage, I decided to inspect the little family, and at the same time check our water supply which remains less than satisfactory until we get the well in the dingle working.

We have to bring water back from the village in old-fashioned milk cans and pump it up to the tanks in the granary. And that's one day's work a week.

But first I wanted to see if the mother squirrel would allow me to get close enough to judge whether her milk supply was sufficient. Already we had realised that if she was to feed four infants properly she, in turn, would have to be properly fed. And indeed, my wife had already provided her with a bowl of milk.

The family were in a plywood fortress my wife had made to protect them from any possible predators and their mum seemed to take me for granted as long as I didn't try to get too close. Naturally, her family were so young that they could not eat solids.

She was very thin but quite strong and healthy and with a

ravenous appetite. She ate as much raw beef as I could cut off a fresh oxhead in two or three minutes.

While this was going on, her children were taking nourishment as though any second it might dry up. But mum seemed all right.

We don't really want grey squirrels in the house because they can be a pest and dangerous, too, particularly in cases where people have indulged in the expensive hobby of using cedar shingles for the roofing of country dwellings.

Under the best conditions cedar is expensive and is not all that long-lasting, but where grey squirrels get into the house they just regard cedar shingles as a great delicacy and will eat any householder out of his or her shingles in a very few meals.

Three or four years ago we had to have all our electric cabling treated with an anti-squirrel preparation and it seems to have worked. Now if we are going to have grey squirrels again in the house it is to be hoped that they will treat us with respect.

My wife had discovered the squirrels while looking for signs of the little pipistrelles who have lived here in increasing quantities in the last few years.

Last night we saw two or three having a meal of fat moths around the light. We are so glad because I always think they are our most beautiful as well as joyful little nocturnal flittermice.

Meanwhile, up in the granary, all is well with the latest family to set up home with us here in the hills.

*   *   *

The other morning I lit the living-room fire for the first time in three months because it had rained during the night (but not enough to do any real good) and it had got so cold that we were shivering.

An hour later, after my wife took the dogs out to exercise them on the mountain, I was hot enough to think of putting the fire out, but it was just as well I didn't because it was soon needed by unexpected strangers.

I heard a gentle tap on the front door and went to open it.

There stood a young couple with a broken dog collar on the end of a lead dangling from the girl's hand.

I asked them what had happened and heard their sad tale. They had been given the pup two weeks previously and the owner had thrown in the pup's collar. It was obviously a well-used one as all the holes were well-worn, particularly the last one which had broken across the hole, allowing the dog to escape.

Apparently it tore away like mad down our drive and straight across our forecourt to vanish downhill on the other side.

The couple were very worried because, they said, every time the dog had seen a sheep that morning it had gone quite crazy and tried to get away. By the way, had I any sheep?

They couldn't apologise enough and, of course, if their wretched pup had done any damage, they'd gladly pay for it.

I already had a pretty good idea what the pup had gone after. Then my wife returned from her walk with the dogs. But before I had time to tell her the sad little story our dogs had picked up a scent and were off with wild yells.

"That's it," I said, "your dog also picked up the scent and is hard on the trail—if it isn't already stuck halfway down a hole. What is your dog, by the way?"

"A pedigree sealyham," the girl said proudly. "But whatever is he after?"

I told her not to worry, that we'd soon catch up with him, and by the noise coming from our two dogs I was evidently right. Then my wife, too, guessed what had happened. "He's been chasing our little foxes," she said, and the girl's face dropped. "Oh dear," she said. "We're so sorry. Are they pets?"

"Not so as you'd notice," was my reply as I went into the saddleroom for the rabbit-spade, and on we went to the old rabbit hole where our dogs were making such a noise, above which we could hear the yelping of a sorely stuck sealyham somewhere down the hole.

While we set about freeing the pup we told the couple about our recently-arrived vixen with cubs and how they had set up home in the burrow.

Getting our dogs out of the way—and I believe that Holly would have freed the stranger by her own efforts if we hadn't been there—it took only a few minutes to cut away the narrow part and free the sealyham which quickly made friends with our two. Then we all returned to the house where the girl dried her pet in front of the fire with a borrowed dog towel. For after a short dash through long grass the pup was soaking wet.

They departed with many thanks—and one of our old collars, in which I had punched a few extra holes to fit the smaller dog.

* * *

We were driving round a bend on the way back from a shopping trip to town when I broke one of the golden rules for drivers that I have been taught from childhood: never swerve sharply to avoid any kind of animal or bird, because you might easily run over a human being instead.

But in this case there were no human beings in sight, nor anything else except two young swallows sitting as good as gold side by side right in our path.

We passed so closely that I couldn't even see if I'd missed them. So I stopped and my wife jumped out, went round to the back and called to me. There were those little birds, still sitting side by side and gazing upward. I looked up, too, and saw two adult swallows swooping by not ten feet away.

Probably the young birds had come to ground because they were tired. Even the most experienced swallows are the clumsiest of birds on their feet, and these were only just fully-fledged. Possibly they hadn't yet learned to take off from a flat surface. Obviously the pair flying around us and squeaking were the parents.

My wife lifted the babies up, one in each hand. Neither made the slightest objection. So she swung up both arms and released them.

Up and away they flew, side by side, between the parents. They flew to a telephone line crossing a field and there all four landed in the same order.

The parents were making quite a noise, and we surmised that the little ones were being instructed in the highway code for migrant birds, with some advice on how to land on telephone lines for good measure.

Presently, other families began to join them on the line and a 20-yard stretch became quite crowded with chattering parents and their offspring, the latter, as at school, all learning the migrants' highway code. So there we left them.

*   *   *

When taking dogs for a mountain walk there are several things to remember:

First, because of the heather and bracken, they need to be fairly long-legged—unless you can keep them to one of the many paths, varying in width from six inches to a foot, made by the mountain sheep.

Holly qualifies easily but Teena, though very active —almost acrobatic in fact—has very short legs as becomes a hunt terrier.

Teena gets soaked to the skin in such conditions if taken over the mountain after heavy dew or during rain. In cold, wet weather very small dogs can suffer on such a walk.

So for an expedition to see our pair of red kites we decided to go by Land-Rover the long way round which takes us to within half a mile of their nest, just a few minutes' walk. And little Teena was wildly excited because she had not been there by this route before.

Much of her excitement was because the first time she went she had put up and chased a wild polecat to its lair.

Naturally it had easily outrun her, but the funny thing was that Holly made no attempt to follow her. She knows all about polecats, how fierce they are but above all the abominable stink they can produce when excited or angry.

We are not saying where the kites' nest is because though the pair has come from either Tregaron or Brecon where sites are well patrolled to guard against thieves in search of rare eggs, this one is not. Except three or four times a week usually by my wife, sometimes accompanied by me as on this occasion.

As we approached very quietly with the dogs mute and at heel (surprising how quickly little Teena has learned all

this), my wife pointed over to the port quarter and there the
kites both were, one of them with something hanging limp
from its claws.

"Down," my wife whispered, and each dog flattened
itself in the narrow sheep-path along which we were walking—which by chance leads directly to the spot.

We had not been seen and the two birds came on fast.
Then, suddenly, near their tree, they both headed down
towards its foot and were lost to sight behind a slight rise.

This meant they were disposing of their prey. A minute
later one bird flew up to the nest, hovered, alighted on the
rim, dipped its head into the nest and flew fast down again.

We knew what that meant. They had hatched out at least
some of their eggs. We had seen enough. Quietly turning,
still followed by silent dogs, we went back to the Land-
Rover and then glanced round. As we did so, one of the
parents flew swiftly up to the tree, stayed there a moment,
and flew down again.

Coasting quietly downhill along that narrow mountain
road, we headed for home, stopping for a drink in the only
pub on the way. And never mentioning kites, as often at
this time of year there are many tourists about.

*   *   *

So far, this summer has not lived up to expectations.

Only a few days ago we had gales, with the rain coming
down in stair-rods.

But our geese were quite unconcerned. They went about
their daily business as usual, sitting in the middle of the
house paddock, flapping and preening and loving it.

Our goose flock is somewhat depleted now. For the
goslings—given to us by neighbours to rear after their
mother had been taken by a fox—have grown enough to go
home to the lonely gander.

Their grateful owners have now built a fox-proof house
for them. And although it looks like a cross between
Alcatraz and the Ritz, at least the youngsters and their dad
will be safe at night.

Patchy, my wife's elderly gelding, and our two goats,

have not been so happy. They have spent days looking
forlornly over their stable doors at the continuous downpour with a mêlée of disgruntled bantams scratching about
in the straw around their feet.

The other day, my wife got up early, and said she was
taking the dogs for a long walk to make up for the last two
days when they had been a bit short changed.

She suggested I put on some wellies and gloves to shift
the enormous nettles growing in the old kitchen garden.
Then she could pick black and red currants when they were
ripe without being stung.

I was wondering what excuse I could give for not doing it.
But half an hour later, after the cats had eaten their breakfast, a rather watery sun appeared. The cats wanted to go
out. So I went with them thinking of my wife tramping
miles with the dogs, and feeling more than a little guilty, I
donned my gloves and boots and sallied forth into the
garden. I grabbed a handful of nettles and heaved. A
shower of fat black caterpillars fell to the ground. I picked
one up and was delighted to see it was the caterpillar of one
of our most beautiful butterflies, the peacock.

I went back to the house to collect a walking stick to pull
forward the nettles gently so as not to disturb them too
much. I couldn't believe it; there were hundreds.

The last time I had seen so many was ten years ago before
we had chickens. I could only think this particular patch was
too dense even for the most intrepid biddy to get through.

I was still standing there when my wife came back from
her walk.

"You haven't exactly hacked your way into the interior,
have you?" she said. I pointed to the caterpillars. "That's
the best excuse yet," she said.

But when she saw them she insisted we put up some
chicken wire to stop the bantams from scoffing the lot.

I sighed, thinking of my peaceful afternoon by the fire
going west, when two friends arrived and seemed more
than willing to help. So it didn't take long. And then I made
myself scarce.

August

Buzzards used to be plentiful and quite a nuisance to game preservers before myxomatosis wiped out most of the rabbit population but up here in the hills today you can often walk a mile or two without ever seeing a buzzard.

Other wild birds and beasts, many of which never ate a rabbit or any other kind of meat, are becoming scarcer and many species seem to have permanently slowed down their breeding habits.

Therefore, going down to look at our well the other day, I was amazed and delighted to hear the mournful cry of a curlew overhead.

I looked up and there it was. It had lowered its landing-gear and was about to alight at the bottom of the well-paddock.

The curlew landed evidently just where it was laying—or had already laid—its eggs, because immediately it disappeared.

I marked the spot in my mind so as to keep the dogs away from the nest, though that did not matter at the moment as my wife had taken them for a mountain walk.

The bottom part of that paddock is boggy and the breeding-spot for several varieties of the local native orchids which I believe are now protected. For that reason we never encourage the dogs to go ploughing about in it.

As I was walking back to the cottage, the curlew got off her nest and flew quite low over my head, again giving her mournful but musical call.

I repeated it as well as I could and she answered me back. Then she wheeled and returned to her nest.

I wondered. The older I get the more I begin to think that

the expression "bird-brained" is not all that fair. Birds not only have intelligence but this curlew at least has politeness plus friendship. I hope she raises her little family successfully and gets them all safely back to Cardigan Bay.

*   *   *

Alice, our Anglo-Nubian goat is a bit of a pain in the neck. We love her dearly but like all her breed she is very temperamental.

All other breeds take to tethers quite happily and Amy our British Saanen is a good example of this. Nevertheless, each animal is tethered to two 56 lb concrete blocks.

This is because goats are expert escape artists and as they browse rather than graze can eat their way through any hedge.

I have never seen anything stop a determined goat and Alice proved the point just two days ago.

She had pulled her blocks 200 yards uphill and was happily feeding on our one poisonous plant, laburnum.

Immediately we realised what had happened, I rang the vet while my wife mixed two tablespoons of Epsom salts with a quarter pint of warm water to dose the animal to help to neutralise the poison.

The vet arrived and did the necessary while my wife prepared to sit up all night with Alice.

About midnight Holly our Rottweiler paid her a visit, worried because she couldn't understand why we were not in bed.

When we first had Alice we were warned she hated dogs. And not surprisingly. Her mother had been killed by one and she herself had only been saved because the local landlord, hearing an appalling noise at one o'clock in the morning, had grabbed his walking stick and done a Seb Coe across the field to belt the assailant over the head.

He had pulled the baby to safety but was too late to save the mother, who was tethered.

A goat should never be left tethered unless under constant supervision, and certainly not at night.

Holly normally loves all the animals on our farm, but she

always gives a wide berth to Alice, having had a few wallops from her very hard head.

Now, however, she realised the goat was in a bad way.

So she began to wash her—first the nose, then over the eyes and down the ears and neck and finally, along the flank.

Alice obviously loved it all and stretched out in the straw exposing her tum for more.

I went back later to find my wife stretched in the straw with Holly cuddled into her left side and Alice tucked under her right arm—all three looking as if they hadn't a care in the world.

Now, the goats are tethered out again, but Alice has four concrete blocks. I wonder how long it will take her to shift that lot.

*   *   *

Though the only pair of swallows we have had this year didn't stay long, we now have two other friendly little summer visitors—a pair of pied flycatchers nesting in one of last year's swallows' nests in the haybay.

They are sharing the haybay with a potter's wasp whose fascinating little mud nest is just under two inches long and shaped exactly like one of those old-fashioned soda-water bottles with a rounded bottom and a thin neck.

This insect is becoming very scarce—probably because badgers eat their nests and contents—and at first we were afraid that the flycatchers would gobble up the potter, which is only a bit more than half the size of a common wasp.

So when the potter started her nest we watched carefully to see if the birds were taking any interest. However, they seemed not to notice her or, if they did, they perhaps decided that discretion was the better part of valour.

These potters fly fast and until they settle on their nest it is difficult to observe them properly. Though they appear to be shining black all over, as soon as they are still the tail can be seen to have two or three bands of brownish yellow.

The breeding process is fascinating. After she has

finished the nest, the potter fills it with caterpillars which she reduces to a state of coma.

She then lays one egg in the neck of the pot, seals the nest and flies away to make another nest. In time the egg hatches out and the larva proceeds to eat the still live caterpillars in the flask. These last until spring when the young wasp emerges from the pot and departs to find a mate.

So there is our potter, coexisting with the two flycatchers whose diet largely consists of flying insects. They hunt from ambush, darting out in a flash at any passing insect, either taking it to the nest or eating it on the spot while awaiting another victim.

They are very small and can manoeuvre like lightning. It is incredible to see.

*   *   *

My wife had gone out for the day, and as the weather was wet I was looking forward to a nice quiet time by the fire with just the dogs and cats for company.

But as Robbie Burns so aptly put it, "The best laid schemes o' mice an' men gang aft a-gley." I was just settling down when the dogs erupted at the window. And when I looked out, some strangers, having been frightened by the revolting sight of our nine-stone Rottweiler Holly baying at them through the glass, were retreating fast back to the gate.

Yelling "Quiet!" to the dogs I went outside to see what they wanted.

They told me they were touring in their caravan but had become hopelessly lost.

Pulling up in our gateway to check the map the children had got out of the car and the eldest girl, aged eight, had opened the caravan door to check on their Siamese cat, which had jumped out and shot off down our field.

They were frantic with worry, asking how on earth they were ever going to get their town-bred cat back again, and would she try to find her way back to Birmingham?

The wife and children were all in tears. The cat had been a

cosseted pet for ten years and now she was lost in the middle of nowhere.

After a long and fruitless search my wife arrived home. She suggested the family put the caravan in our field and stay the night. She took the children's mind off their troubles by taking them around with her to feed the banties, geese, and goats. Then she gave them rides round the fields on Patchy the gelding who, while not relishing his new role as a glorified seaside donkey, behaved throughout like the gentleman he is.

After another search and a late dinner my wife called us to come out and look at the bats, and the children were enthralled, never having seen such creatures before.

Suddenly we heard the unmistakable yowl of a fed-up Siamese, and out of the darkness stalked the most beautiful, elegant cat I've ever seen. She leaped into her mistress's arms complaining bitterly, giving every indication of a cat who had tasted the wild life and didn't want any more, thank you.

She was brought into the house to be fed and after a good wash she settled in front of the fire with the dogs.

The family left the next morning with a complaining Siamese firmly shut in her travelling crate.

* * *

Talking to a fisherman in our local he immediately complained about the spread of the mink.

In the free state, these tough little animals of the *mustela* tribe (it includes the badger, otter, polecat and weasel) are more predatory than any of their relatives and far more dangerous because they are small, speedy and breed just as quickly as stoat or weasel. In fact, in sufficient numbers they can destroy the most valuable fishery far quicker than the otter ever did.

One very early morning I got down to the river and chose a spot to wait and watch. Shortly before daylight I was rewarded. Near the far bank a gleaming white body suddenly snaked out of the water, something silver crosswise in its mouth: a half-pound trout.

Behind her in single-line appeared four half-grown mink. They surrounded the mother on a stone on the bank and voraciously fell to. She just sat and watched them.

I imagined that when they had finished, they would hunt again for more, because it wasn't much of a meal for four hungry youngsters. However, there was no wait for cleaning whiskers or anything else because a car hove in sight, accelerating to get over a humpback bridge.

In a second those beautiful creatures were in the water, swimming fast downstream away from the bridge. It was almost daylight now. I looked . . . and there was not a morsel of fish left on that stone.

*   *   *

We had just started our breakfast when we heard the first signs of trouble.

Suddenly an almighty clamour was set up by the geese, Albert, Vicky and the gosling who is now half-grown with the same grey and white colouring as Albert but who hasn't been named yet because we still don't know its sex.

We ran outside, and at once saw the cause of the commotion: the geese had arrived for their morning bath, expecting as usual to enjoy the water in all its limpid tranquillity. But there, splashing about in the middle with an old and much punctured plastic soccer ball, was our ebullient young Rottweiler bitch, Holly.

Seeing us, Holly got out of the pool with the water-filled ball still in her mouth. Whereupon Albert went for her at speed, using both legs and wings, and making a noise more like that of a mad bull.

Deciding that discretion was the best policy, Holly jumped over a stone wall into the west paddock, knowing that Albert, who is huge and heavy, would need at least a 50-yard runway to clear such an obstacle. But having seen the invader off, Albert trumpeted with the voice of triumph and so did his family, running and flapping forward to congratulate him.

We returned to the house to finish our breakfast, accompanied by Holly with the ball, when little Teena the terrier decided to have some fun.

She made a leap for the ball and a tussle for possession developed. In no time water was squirting out of the puncture holes all over the place.

After putting the dogs outside we went back to the table to continue our breakfast of bacon and eggs. But not a morsel was left, thanks to the cats which had left their tell-tale footprints all over the empty plates and a knocked-over milk jug.

There was nothing we could do except make light of it and cook another breakfast, which this time we managed to consume without interruption.

* * *

I had noticed the dead rabbit when I looked out of the bedroom window at the start of the day.

It was a young adult doe, the mother of four half-grown bunnies living in a nearby bramble thicket.

Obviously, I thought, it must have been shot and badly wounded by a hunter, and had died on the way home.

It would make a good meal for the cats that night.

So I set off to collect it for the pot, pausing only to proffer a treat to Patchy, my wife's old gelding, who is now getting a bit long in the tooth but is none the worse for that, bless him, and is ever ready to come ambling up for a bit of chocolate.

Our three cats, seeming to sense that this little trek would result in a special treat for them, accompanied me in frisky fashion across the paddock to where the dead doe lay.

Back in the house, I was dealing with the rabbit when my wife, who had been out with the dogs, returned. She had seen four people with guns and a couple of lurchers in the rough paddock bottom which years ago housed all sorts of small game, rabbits, snipe, woodcock and pheasant, all good eating for a hungry family be it the landlord's, farmer's, gipsy's, or poachers.

Now all it contains is a few pair of snipe and a few rabbit families. Plus weasels, stoats and polecats which are not of interest to the sporting gun, or at least they shouldn't be.

To put her mind at rest I said I'd have a look if she would put my rabbit on to cook for the moggies' suppers, and I set out with Teena the terrier who would flush out and catch anything that was not 100 per cent fit.

We had only just arrived when I saw someone else had obviously had the same idea: a large polecat, so intent on his hunt that he didn't seem to see us, was slinking towards one of the many bramble thickets, though fortunately, not the one I was making for.

Clipping Teena's lead on, I went quietly away in the opposite direction leaving him, hopefully, to find a meal for his family.

We eventually found our four bunnies where expected, all very much alive and perfectly well. So Teena and I took ourselves off home again.

* * *

Our neighbour's hay had been harvested. A contractor had mown the five-acre field and, because the neighbour was short of barn space, the 55 bales were stacked in our haybay.

But the busy contractor had been in a hurry and the baling had been done while the hay was still slightly "green", a lack of hot, dry sunshine not helping matters.

So I was not surprised that when my wife went to the bay a couple of days later to inspect the contents by shoving a hand between two bales, she found that the hay was steaming wet and heating up.

She gave the neighbour a ring and soon he arrived and the affected bales were placed on end on the concrete floor to dry out.

Soon they had cooled and it was necessary just to keep an eye on the others in case they began to heat up too.

It was as well that we did. For the very next day when my wife was in the haybay making sure all was well she heard a faint cheeping noise coming from behind the stack.

And a quick search disclosed a dead bantam pullet, Harriet, her neck obviously having been broken by a falling bale, surrounded by eight chicks no more than three days old, all yelling away at the top of their tiny voices.

We brought them into the house, putting them in a box and giving them warm milk which they managed perfectly even though it must have been the first drink of their lives. Then I put some breakfast cereal into a pestle, pounded it a bit and that was that. Less than half an hour later there was none left and the tiny chicks were all huddled together asleep in a corner of the box.

But there was another problem. They would need a heated pen for three or four days and we hadn't got one.

Then my wife remembered Henrietta, the dead mother's sister, who seemed to have been sitting on four eggs for a long time. So we took one egg out, put in a chick—and Henrietta immediately began to mother it, clucking away contentedly. One by one the others were introduced . . . and the problem was solved. Soon they were all rushing around their proud foster mum, having a lovely time.

Of course, we'll miss Harriet but that was a minor disaster that can happen on any farm; thank heavens that at least my wife's sensitive ears saved the chicks.

Bantams have a tiresome habit of sneaking off somewhere, laying a clutch of eggs and hatching them out undisturbed, bringing them proudly in as soon as they can hop.

The miracle is that these chicks lasted so long without any food except hayseeds they could pick up for themselves.

And as things turned out, how lucky it was that the hay had heated up. They would certainly otherwise have died of cold.

*　　*　　*

Some time ago I mentioned a breeding pair of red kites within 10 (or 50 if you like, I am not saying where) miles from this farm.

Those birds tried out our predator bird-table last winter two or three times but gave it up because there were always at least two ravens and four or five carrion crows (we have no hooded crows hereabouts, thank goodness) on the premises, who objected strongly. And by now all our birds respect one another's bird-tables.

Before we gave up a paddock to be the predators' table there was sometimes a problem when the small bird-table, capable of accommodating between 200 and 300 assorted small birds, was raided by predators. This used to be my cue to rush out with all dogs, yelling. Predators took off instantly while many small birds took no notice at all. But now that the predators have their own table they never come near the small birds' premises.

But on Wednesday there was nothing down there but bare oxskulls, because Thursday is our day for putting down fresh ones. The word had got out on the bush telegraph that this was so. Our regular customers never bother on Wednesday. But this had evidently not reached the red kites, who have always been *persona non grata* to our local ravens, and who happened to be passing overhead.

I was in my workroom when a terrific racket broke out on the forecourt where my wife had just put out food for our bantams. The hens were all squawking madly. So, thinking something dire was about to happen, I rushed out with the guard-pack at my heels, both yelling madly.

The dogs nearly upset my wife and did indeed upset her corn-measure all over the place. There, flying over the fence and also yelling his head off, was Cocky the bantam cockerel. Thirty yards lower down, investigating the skulls, were two kites.

Cocky was nearly there, flying fast, hitting the ground every ten yards to take off again (I think he finds this method of flying a bit faster than sustained flight), crowing his head off, red comb angrily gleaming, bright feathers furiously flashing.

My wife was sitting on the dry-stone wall, laughing helplessly. The hens and four chicks were vigorously attacking the spilt corn, and those kites took off as though all hell were at their forked tails.

By this time our two pairs of resident ravens were also on the job, not to mention half a dozen carrion crows. Instantly assessing the situation, they flew fast after the vanishing kites; but I am glad to say they could not overtake them.

The crows returned. My wife put out some lumps of meat (even on a Wednesday) on their paddock. Cocky strutted proudly back, to be met halfway by his wives and children, all squawking in loud praise. And I returned to the blessed peace and quiet of my workroom.

* * *

It has been a very good year for soft fruits and our black-currant bushes are bowed down with luscious, plump berries.

The two weeks' warm, dry weather we had in May set the fruit beautifully and all the rain hasn't done it any harm.

But since at this altitude things are much later than down at river level, only this week did we decide to start picking.

Before we could begin, however, I had to clear away the long grass and nettles from around the bushes. So while my wife went into the house for a couple of colanders, I collected the scythe and set to.

Enjoying my task, I suddenly realised I was no longer alone; a small army of pickers were following my progress. A family of blackbirds—parents and three young—and half a dozen bullfinches, those scourges of market garden-ers, were tucking in for all they were worth on the bushes I had cleared.

I called to my wife that if she wanted any currants she had better come quickly or they would all be gone!

She duly appeared with the dogs and Puss, our black Persian cat. The birds, spotting the cat, retreated to the trees and my wife and I started picking. Soon both our bowls were full. Our attention was drawn to Puss: crouched, tail swishing, two bushes away. Just as she was about to pounce, I yelled. She jumped round and glared at me before stalking off in a very marked manner.

We noticed that one of the branches on the bush that Puss had been watching was bending slowly down. We watched fascinated as a tiny fieldmouse climbed to the end of a thin, heavily laden branch and swung upside down.

He was closely followed by two more who, staying top-side, proceeded to the very tip of the branch, sat up and had a quick look round. Then, working methodically from the top, they started to bite through the stems of the bunches of currants.

As they fell to the ground, the rest of the family gathered the harvest and carted it into the long grass I hadn't yet cut. It was a prodigious feat as some of those bunches must have weighed more than the mice.

We filled four more colanders before deciding to call it a day and leave the birds and fieldmice to have a feed and, in the case of the mice, stock up their larder.

* * *

When I was a small boy my aunt Gertrude gave me (with much good advice) a book titled *The Country*, and published by the Religious Tract Society in 1790.

It contains quite a lot of very interesting facts, one of which is illustrated by the following verse, quoted by Old Michael, the gardener, to young Maurice, a schoolboy.

The talk was of nettles and young Maurice said: "Nettles. I cannot abide them. They are no use to anyone, and they sting." His moral mentor proceeded to enlighten the boy by quoting the following verse:

> Tender handed touch a nettle
> And it stings you for your pains,
> Grasp it like a man of mettle
> And it soft as silk remains.
> So it is with vulgar natures,
> Use them kindly they rebel
> But be rough as nutmeg graters,
> And the rogues obey you well.

Michael went on to tell of the numerous creatures which made good use of nettles, which also made admirable "porridge". Certainly it is a useful green vegetable when the tender tops are cooked like spinach.

The other day I went out with a scythe and cut most of the seven-foot high nettles there and spread them out on the forecourt to catch the sun.

By sunset they were limp enough to have lost their sting.

So we let Patchy the horse and the two goats on to the forecourt where they fell on them ravenously.

I read the little rhyme of Old Michael to a ten-year-old boy who was visiting us, but before I had time to enlarge on it, he was out into the New Garden to put it to the test on some nettles I had left standing strong and high.

I shouted to him to stop, but it was too late. He yelled and came running back to the house, with badly stung hands. If I had had time I would have told him that to do this trick safely he had to grasp the *top* of the nettle, not the tougher bits lower down.

*   *   *

A spin-off from our find and rescue the other week of eight motherless bantam chicks in the haybay was the discovery of a pair of spotted flycatchers nesting on a beam.

They seem to have several youngsters in quite an advanced state but this is hardly surprising since the haybay is well ventilated and quite weatherproof. They were therefore unaffected by the torrential rains that have plagued us on and off this summer.

It is unfortunate that the last few days of brilliant sunshine did not come a fortnight or three weeks ago. They would have added thousands of pounds to the value of the hill farmers' hay-crop. But there it is: this seems to be a real Indian summer—wonderful for holidaymakers but not much use to those who live in the hills.

One thing the fine weather *has* done is to bring out flies and the spotted flycatchers are having a wonderful harvest, just when they need it most. For their four fledglings are now sufficiently feathered to look abominably untidy, but at least they can fly in a fashion and are busily learning how to catch their staple diet.

Their parents, wise in the ways of flies, almost certainly chose their nesting place with this in mind. The east end of the haybay faces the morning sun, which means that the wall soon gets quite hot.

Flies love this and so do the flycatchers. One of them will sit on top of a two-foot high weed and wait until a bluebottle is just about to settle on it for a toe-warming session. Then there is a lightning blur of feathers, and—snap! One fly less, and the bird has resumed its perch on the weed.

Looking out of the kitchen window the other morning about an hour after sunrise I noticed not one but three flycatchers hanging about the haybay's east wall with the sun just beginning to warm up the top half.

I went out on to the lane and walked along to the haybay gate. In order not to disturb the birds at their lesson I moved stealthily down the fence until I could get a view of the east wall.

At first I couldn't see any of the youngsters but the little hen made two flights, landing briefly on the ground before flying up to her weed. Evidently her young were still grounded and I wondered: they had probably fluttered from their beam where the nest is and landed safely but how, since the beam is at least eleven feet high, would they get back unaided?

I needn't have worried because one of them quite neatly flew up on to a slightly lower weed than the hen's. Facing the right way too, with a clear view of the wall.

Suddenly a large bluebottle landed on the stone within three feet of the learner, who launched himself at it. He scored an inner at six o'clock which sent the fly off in quite a leisurely manner—too leisurely as it happened. The hen made a swift dart at it and engulfed it.

This went on for half an hour and I'm sure that all four fledglings were on the job because at one point three of them went for the same fly, collided in mid-air, lost their victim and fell to the ground in a tangle.

After half an hour the telephone rang and since my wife was out with the dogs I had to leave the birds to answer it.

When I went back later to see if the youngsters had got back to the nest, I found them all sitting happily in a line along their beam.

September

After a violent night of gales and torrential rain a quiet, still morning saw us outside ruefully surveying our kitchen roof, one corner of which was completely devoid of slates.

These had been dragged off by a fallen branch from one of the ash trees and as we pondered the problem we suddenly realised that something else was wrong . . . it was just too quiet.

Then we realised why: the stream was silent.

Ever since we've been here, except in drought, the noise of the water rushing over the rocks, into the duck-pond and out again under the drive has added its own friendly background music to all our backdoor activities.

The storms of the night should have filled the stream bank high but something was stopping its flow and there was only a trickle.

We went to have a look at our neighbour's field, where the spring which feeds out stream rises, to see if anything was blocking it at source. But instead of a field there was a sizeable lake. All that was holding it back was one of our Welsh dry-stone walls.

Something would have to be done and quickly. The blockage was obviously in the tunnel which carries the stream under the road and into our garden.

This, made long before tarmac was invented, is constructed of large flat stone slabs forming a V shape with even bigger slabs across the top. Had one of those slabs slipped after all these years?

Suddenly Teena the terrier, who had been splashing about in the little pools, disappeared into the tunnel. We could hear her whining excitedly. And suddenly her rump and wildly wagging tail appeared. My wife grabbed it and pulled, and out came Teena hanging grimly on to a branch.

We both tugged hard and as the branch started to come free it dawned on us that once we removed the blockage there would be a massive deluge and we were in direct line for a thorough soaking. So we leapt sideways as the branch and a large bundle of twigs came free.

Unfortunately the dogs were not so quick and ended up in the duck-pond. Happily nothing was hurt but their pride, and once on dry land they dived at the bundle of twigs which had come to rest against the bank. Out scrambled two very wet, very cross grey squirrels. They leapt up the bank scolding loudly and vanished over the other side.

The tree in which they had their drey had been blown down and their home had been swept straight into the culvert under the road and had become so firmly wedged that they had been unable to claw their way out.

Well at least they were alive, though homeless. And there is ample time for them to rebuild their quarters—and for us to repair ours—before the cold weather sets in.

*   *   *

The relationship between our geese, Victoria and Albert, is nothing like that which existed between their nearest namesakes.

"Dearest Albert we must never have any secrets from each other," our former Queen was said to have shyly whispered to her love, thereby informing him that he was free to examine any secret papers relating to affairs of State, and advice her on them.

But if our Victoria could talk her consort would doubtless be told in no uncertain manner to "do as I say and do it quickly or you'll feel the sharp edge of my beak." Not that Albert minds being goose-pecked. In fact he always seems only too pleased to carry out Victoria's orders.

The other day they were in the stableyard and I was watching them from the adjoining forecourt wall. Victoria was lying down on top of the muckheap and Albert was at the foot of it, standing on one bandy leg as if keeping watch over her.

Then, quite suddenly, she set up a loud cackle, obviously saying something like, "Stop standing there on one leg you stupid gander . . . come up here and sit down beside me."

Obediently, Albert did as he was told, giving her a gentle peck on the neck and then looking at me, hoping perhaps for a bit of sympathy. I gave it by filling their water bowl from the rain barrel and immediately they rushed down to enjoy a thorough wash.

The geese can be alarming to visitors because they always run at them honking loudly with wings outstretched.

They sleep on the forecourt under my workroom window where they have a fine night view of our drive gate and the front door. And woe betide any nocturnal visitor because they are forever on the alert and run to the attack with a maximum of noise, which causes the dogs to give tongue as well, a combined row that would put a regiment to flight.

Yesterday morning Puss, our black Persian, was walking across the forecourt to tap on the living-room window and request her morning milk in the kitchen, when for some reason or other both geese attacked her with maximum speed and noise.

The reason for the assault is a mystery. For Puss would never think of going for a goose. But the poor creature didn't stop to think about that. She made first for the window, then realised that the sill was well in reach of the hard beaks of her pursuers. So in mid-gallop she turned left and at full speed made for the safety of the willow tree by the drive gate.

She got there about six inches ahead of two wide-open beaks and shot up the tree to the first branch, about eight feet high.

She still wasn't quite safe because by jumping with wings flapping wildly the furious pair could still reach her. Missing one dangerous beak by an inch, she made for the top branches but not until I went out to feed them did they allow her to come down again.

Puss was lucky to escape for those beaks can be dangerous weapons indeed. As if to illustrate this, Albert recently pecked a two inch deep hole in the concrete in front of our window—without causing any damage to his beak.

Why did he venture on such a useless task? Goodness knows, unless it was to show off to that bossy wife of his.

*   *   *

Malcolm our woodman arrived the other day with a welcome load of oak and beech logs—the start of our winter woodpile.

Unfortunately (for us not for him) he now has a newfangled hydraulic tip-up trailer for his tractor which is far too big to manoeuvre into our forecourt. So instead of throwing the wood over the wall by hand and complaining about the state of the country and the price of hay, he just pushed a button and the entire load was tipped right outside . . . right in front of the gate.

The wood couldn't possibly stay there, because at any moment we were expecting a couple of tons of coal to keep our home fires burning until Christmas—and the coalman would need to drive through the gate to deliver this load. There was nothing to do but to shift the lot by hand. So we set to.

As it happened, we had only just started when he arrived, but cheerful and obliging as ever, he carted his delivery sack by sack to the shed.

Later that evening my wife put the dogs out as usual and called to me to come outside.

She was obviously excited. So I trotted out to see what was up. There in the middle of the forecourt sat a pair of toads; fat, squat, ungainly beasts which some would call ugly, which nevertheless have the most beautiful red eyes.

They regarded us solemnly for a few minutes, then turned slowly around and crawled back to the woodpile and vanished underneath it. They could only have come with the wood.

Toads like to lie up during the day and a woodpile is a good a place as any—in fact, better since lots of nocturnal insects seek similar daytime situations, thus offering the toads a continuous food supply.

We decided to move the remaining wood and catch the little creatures and transfer them to the permanent winter pile where they would be safe.

Now we wonder whether they will stay. We hope so because of the vast quantities of harmful insects they eat.

But toads have a very well developed homing instinct, and will travel miles to their spawning grounds. And so since the wood came from only one and a half miles away, it does seem doubtful.

We will just have to wait and see if the toads consider the woodpile their home and remain here, or if they will make their way back down the valley whence they were so rudely, albeit unknowingly, transported by our woodman.

* * *

Sun was promised for the forenoon, with a falling glass later in the day, possibly accompanied by local storms. But this has been the forecast so many times in the last six months that we took no notice and soon after breakfast, took the dogs on their leads out for a nice sunny walk.

We were more than halfway home when the wind changed to the west, got much colder and presently there came the angry roar of thunder.

As a few huge drops of rain began to patter down we made for a gate, with our farm visible a hundred yards below it.

Then came a roar of thunder dead overhead and a flash of forked lightning between us and our cottage. While I shut the gate behind us my wife whipped off leads and collars; the leads because they end in steel choke-chains, the collars because they are lined with brass studs and any kind of metal can act as a lightning conductor.

Ever since a farmer friend had one of his sheep dogs killed by lightning striking its collar we have always let our dogs run free in a thunderstorm.

But then came a diversion from Teena, the little hunt terrier. This was the first time she had been out in a heavy thunderstorm with lightning grounding itself so dangerously near.

Immediately I took her collar off she set up a yelling never before heard and crouched down as if in terror.

As she doesn't weigh very much my wife picked her up and carried her home, where we hung up the leads and collars and dried the dogs.

Teena, however, was still all adrift, running first to her mistress, then to me, then to where the leads and collars were hanging up.

The penny dropped for my wife. She got up and took down Teena's collar, putting it on the little terrier.

"She thought we were going to send her back to the lost dogs' home. You may remember, she had no collar and—as a hunt terrier—had probably never worn one until, on the way home after getting her, we bought her one," she said. "And it only gets taken off in the bath."

The storm still raged and the noise was terrific but the little dog cared not a whit; from one to the other of us she ranged, jumping on to laps to say how glad she was that we were not, after all, going to send her back to the home. That collar was her sign that she belonged, and we loved her all the more for it.

* * *

Where we had gone I will not say but it was to see if we could spot a member of the chough family.

This is of the *Corvidae* comprising, in all, the raven, carrion crow, hooded crow, rook, jackdaw, magpie, jay and chough. The chough is regarded as the most harmless of the eight and is the only one which is a shoreline dweller.

It is very rare now save in the west coasts of Scotland and Wales with a few survivors in Cornwall. He is a very distinctive crow because, although his plumage is shiny black, his beak and legs are reddish-yellow.

So there we were, over 90 miles from home at the edge of a 100 ft cliff and the silence was audible. We waited and within ten minutes they appeared. Four birds coasted above the cliff before descending to the shore.

But easily in the sunlight we had seen their legs—bright red at that distance. They were choughs—parents and two

children. Our day had been made. And hence the secrecy.
For there are still egg-collectors about.

As the choughs were too far away to photograph, we
decided to walk along the cliff top to a spot where my wife
had spotted a commotion in the water. Fortunately there
was a tallish cliff-top bush at that point and we were able to
squat behind it and look down without being seen from
below.

The sea was nearly as calm as a millpond. Half a dozen
seals were swimming about in the water. Five or six more
were sunning themselves on rocks. And as we watched, two
of them, on a large flat rock, were making the fondest
gestures to each other.

It was of course the mating season. And from the two on
the flat rock there came a continuous burble, not of barks
but of content.

Then they slipped into the water, nudging each other,
diving and shooting out of it, having a marvellous morning.

But suddenly some people in a speedboat hurtled round
the corner, saw the seals and stopped, so that they too
could watch. But there was no longer anything to see. The
seals had disappeared.

* * *

We love our bantams one and all, not just for their good
looks and endearing (sometimes) ways, but also because
they lay delicious little free-range eggs all over the place.

Well, for some days the egg yield had been slowly but
remorselessly falling, until we were seven or eight down on
the usual figure. It looked as if those missing eggs were
being used to feed a fast-growing family of some sort.

We knew that it was not a day-feeding family either,
because we had kept a close eye on a certain nest that was
being regularly used by three bantams. So we decided to
share an all-night watch on that nest, armed with a shotgun.

And in her half of the first night's watch my wife, who
had a powerful torch with her, found out who the culprits
were. She came stamping up the stairs in great excitement,
waking me up as she sat down puffing on the bed.

Hearing a slight rustling, she had switched on the torch and in its beam she saw very clearly, two weasels, each one with an egg. Seemingly a sire and dam, the bigger one was carrying his egg in both arms and making short runs, each one of five or six feet, then putting the egg down for a short rest, before repeating the exercise.

The mother had her egg in one arm clasped to her chest and was hopping along on three legs; a bit more efficiently than her husband but of course, slower. And there were several little ones helping as children will, getting under the feet of the parents.

Of course, we wouldn't dream of shooting them because the little weasel, as any farmer knows, is a useful small but deadly beast to keep the stackyard and granary free from rats.

I felt that a short sharp shock would fill the bill and settle the matter, and the occasion came two nights later.

We were keeping watch together at about midnight, listening to the snuffles of Patchy the horse grazing nearby, when my wife switched on the light . . . and there we saw a weasel at the nest.

Immediately I let out a stentorian blast of sound—"Hiya, Catsmeat. Come and get it!" There was an answering snort from Patchy, the thunder of hooves almost over the nest, and the instantaneous disappearance of the weasel. Patchy crashed through his doorway, to stamp for a bit of corn, which of course he got. Since then we have lost no more eggs.

* * *

After three summers without a good crop of blackberries, hazel nuts, beechmast and so on, this year there were signs that if we had another week or two of warm sunshine we could have a record crop of everything.

The rowan trees are all red with bright berries— thankfully not blown off by high winds. In this case let's hope that the equinoctial gales, due in a few days, will not be too violent.

There is also a very heavy crop of elderberries coming on

nicely, while I have never seen so many sloes on our blackthorns. They and the elderberries are quite wind-proof. So we and the birds can rely on them, and their winter food will be all right.

Yesterday we were out blackberrying and on the way down to the east boundary cracked a few of the very many hazelnuts that grow in our hedges. Ten days ago those nuts were full of soft centres which have now turned into nuts, but not yet quite ripe. With another ten days of warm weather there will be a huge crop.

Curiously, though, we haven't seen many grey squirrels at our level of between 900 and 1,150 feet above sea level. The swallows have all moved much lower down the valley where they are already packing along the telephone lines prior to emigrating.

Yesterday afternoon it was balmy with bright sun and no wind. We went down to the blackberries with the dogs and our little polydactyl (many fingered) black Tom cat. He was really out in the wilds for the first time in his life, and revelling in it.

Suddenly there was a yell from him. At first we could not tell where he was. Already on the way down from the house he had climbed a tree, not more than ten feet high, and had been swaying wildly to and fro on the top branch which was bending like a fishing rod. He was clinging to it with every one of his 26 claws. So all I had to do was to pull down a lower branch until I could pick him off.

But he jumped from my arms, landing between two thick blackberry branches, fast held by thorns and scared of using anything but his voice. Luckily, I had brought a sickle down to cut a way through the thicker patches and a few swipes soon freed him. After that, evidently thinking that both episodes had been my doing, he avoided me and went to sit down beside my wife.

As to the blackberries, an hour's picking yielded us nearly 6 lb of beautiful ripe berries. There must be 5 lb or 6 lb left in the same patch. So there will be no fruit shortage in this household for some time to come.

*　　*　　*

I have commented this year on the increase in the grey
squirrel population up here in the hills.

In the last few years the local squirrels had virtually
vanished, due to the almost total failure of the nut-crop.

They had not died, but departed to local towns and
villages where they could at least pick up a sort of living out
of dustbins and so forth.

I reckon those village and town-dwelling squirrels had
learned on their grapevine of the strange plentitude of nuts
in their old bailiwick and returned.

What is not so easy to account for is the fact that in the last
fortnight we must have seen ten or so baby rabbits—
something we had not seen for years.

Our rabbits today are mostly brush-dwellers and no
longer use their old burrows or warrens, but a brushwood
rabbit is more vulnerable to four-legged predators than
those living underground. And consequently fewer of their
progeny have survived.

Something has changed that and I can't think what.

This year there are more than twice the number of young
rabbits than we have seen about in the last ten or 12 years.
And we hope that they will prosper because I was never the
kind of farmer who went about saying: "I was ruined by
rabbits."

The other day I was thinking about this, sitting in a warm
patch of sun with Teena the hunt terrier lying peacefully
beside me. About 20 yards away four baby rabbits, just
about capable of getting about and nibbling at a bit of
grass—and likewise enjoying the sun—were playing a few
yards from the patch of brushwood in which was obviously
their nest.

Outside sat a very large doe, warily on guard, and
keeping an extra wary eye on Teena and me. I was not
carrying a gun or anything that even looked like one, such
as a shepherd's thorn-stick. None the less she wasn't quite
happy.

Then one of those tiny rabbits hopped up to within six
inches of Teena's nose. The little beast sat up on its hind-
quarters, brushing finger and thumb of one hand across its
nose.

Teena opened one eye, then two, but still making no sound poked out her neck towards the brave little investigator.

It hopped one pace forward and stuck out its nose. Teena lengthened her neck the necessary two inches, and they actually touched noses. Next moment they would have been playing.

Obviously this was going to be an utterly peaceful mission on both sides. But Mum thought differently. She gave three enormous thumps on the ground with her hind feet, that even I could hear.

And by the time that Teena had been able to retract her neck there wasn't a rabbit to be seen anywhere.

But I had noticed that the doe had stood aside from the nest until all the little ones had vanished. Then she vanished too.

Poor little dog! She was quite disconsolate for the next few minutes.

*   *   *

We look after our hedgehogs carefully, because they are valuable animals to have around.

Indeed, thanks to them we have no snails and very few slugs. Thanks also to the badgers I have not seen one wasp except one vague wanderer that got into the Land-Rover's cab one afternoon when we had been down at sea level.

But what I have seen up here is a hedgehog carefully cleaning up the survivors of a wasps' nest that a badger had destroyed early one morning.

Two or three weeks ago my wife, having put the dogs out for their late-night runaround, came in quite excited, saying that Holly was bringing in a hedgehog—a fat one. Well, we did not want this; it was still summer and the dormant season for hedgies was still weeks away, whatever the weather seemed to indicate.

We went out and there were the dogs; Holly in front with a huge hedgehog in her mouth. And her mouth is one that the highest-trained retriever would be proud to have.

She can actually carry eggs in it without breaking them

and once brought in two together from the bantam pen without cracking either.

Holly dropped her burden gently to the ground. It uncurled itself, got on to its ridiculously short legs, and had a look around.

Slowly and completely unafraid, it approached the stone step up into the house—on the right-hand side where we put milk down for hedgehogs if they seem to be asking for some—and came to a halt.

My wife went in to get a saucerful, having first told the dogs *sit*, and then *stay*.

In seconds they were both sitting in a semi-circle within three feet of that hedgehog—which remained standing —while the dogs stayed seated. Both had their mouths wide open and were grinning broadly.

My wife returned with the milk and put it down under hedgy's nose. He (or she) immediately started to drink —until the saucer was empty.

Since then, this routine has been repeated two or three times a week, the latest taking place late one night last week. And we are wondering how long it will be before they go into hibernation.

So far, this year's seasons have gone totally haywire —even to the point of having our equinoctial gales days too early—although that may have been only a dummy run and we could still get them in all their fury even tomorrow.

But it is nowhere near hibernation weather yet, and from now until then we may be faced with the dogs bringing in that hedgehog for his nocturnal sustenance every time we let them out for their goodnight runaround.

* * *

Our summer has departed with the swallows. So now we have to wait and prepare for winter and I personally am not looking forward to it.

As I write the temperature is 40F—the coldest registered here since mid-spring—and it has hardly stopped raining for three days with the wind always from half to full gale force. It has veered about wildly and last night went due north, which we had not anticipated.

In the same three days the barometer has dropped a whole inch and now stands at 28½, whereas in the previous eighteen or so days it had varied very little, staying between 29.4 and 29.6.

It was in the middle of the night while we were in bed, with the wind and rain at its worst when bedlam broke loose outside.

Chucking a couple of mackintoshes over us, my wife grabbed up the powerful lamp while I loaded a couple of shotguns, one of which was my old Greener single-shot as it throws a very heavy load for a very long way. The other is a three-shot repeater which I handed to my wife to carry for me for immediate use if necessary.

The main racket was coming from two looseboxes, one of which contains Patchy, my wife's gelding who sleeps with Rebecca and Naomi the two donkeys. They were stamping and snorting, all three trying to stick their heads through the lower half-door (the upper is left open at night except in winter) trying to tell us what was happening. But seeing us with guns and a searchlight, they calmed down.

We then looked over the half-door into the other loosebox which contains geese and bantams, all busy wind-flapping, honking and clucking.

It was impossible to count them all, but there were no corpses lying about. So we plodded up through mud to see if the haybay door was properly shut. It was, and by this time we were both wet and horrid cold, the guns were wet, and now that the animals were quiet all we could hear was the sound of the downpour plus the northerly wind blowing nearly at storm force.

We went back to bed again after leaving the hospitality light burning in front of the cottage, plus lights shining through the two kitchen windows.

I surmised that we had been visited by the two or three remaining of the eight European wolves that had escaped from the Cardigan Wildlife Park after killing 30 of the park's own animals, including rare breeds of deer, sheep and goats.

If so, they had been foiled by the racket kicked up by our beasts. Or perhaps our prompt appearance with searchlight and two guns, both of us in shiny macs, had been enough to make them flee.

So, after a restorative hot toddy, we went to bed, rather pleased to have proved to our animals, and to ourselves, that we can move promptly when necessary.

*   *   *

We were on our way home from town when we decided to have a drink at a little country pub.

We bundled in with Holly the Rottweiler. Our dogs are trained to be kind to publicans, policemen, postmen and parsons.

They are also trained to behave themselves in pubs by lying under a table or, if no table, under our chairs.

As one does over a pint, we got into conversation. Within minutes an old local mentioned that his wife had recently bought a young donkey and he thought there was something wrong with her hooves. She was not being ridden and her feet were getting a bit long in the hoof, so much so that they were already turning up at the tips.

I have often seen donkey's hooves eight or nine inches long and turned up at the ends like a pair of Turkish slippers—but when they get that bad it can be a major operation. I asked where the donkey was and the man said just round the corner. Would I care to have a look?

Five minutes later there was the donkey outside the door with a nice light burning bright. We had a blacksmith's searching knife and a pair of hoof clippers in the toolbox because in my younger days I could forge a shoe to fit and put it on to stay.

So, with the help of a woolly scarf I was able to hold the foot in the right position while my wife got busy with the searching knife (to clean up the bottom or inside of the hoof and then clip the rim down to the required length). She made a neat job of it.

Then came the question. How much did I want? Now when I started taking an interest in this sort of thing a good blacksmith would charge between six and eight old pennies, depending on how bad the hooves were. In our case this had been no problem; not more than a little more than half an inch had to come off. But in worse cases it can be an operation.

Nowadays the stock charge for performing such an operation if £3 to £4. Having grown up in the days when you could get a stout cob shod on all fours for anything between four and five old shillings (20 to 25 new pence), it is difficult for me to understand today's charges for the same service —between £7 and £8.

But there it is. I was asked how much I wanted. I replied nothing at all as my wife enjoyed having a bit of practice.

Then drinks were offered but I refused as there were still over 40 miles to get home. And I would not care to lose my licence. So my wife had a large dry sherry and I a tomato juice.

After long farewells and a piece of chocolate for Holly, away we went and soon arrived home.

But when we got into the garage and I turned on the main lights, what do you think we found in the glove compartment of the car? A half-bottle of rum. So we drank to the health of that little jennyass in a hot rum toddy before going to bed.

* * *

The latter part of September has been far cooler than normal—much more like an average mid-October. So for a week now we have kept the living-room fire going, banking it up each night ready for revival in the morning.

Already the trees are changing colour, though not yet shedding their leaves. Except the ash, which loses some with every autumnal gale.

As for the wild fruit trees and bushes, this year's blackberry crop must be a record, much to the delight of countless birds. And there are excellent crops of hazel nuts and beechmast for the grey squirrels and various members of the mouse family (including a small family of black rats nearby).

There is also an enormous crop of sloes, which will be taken full advantage of by countless birds and quadrupeds.

Meanwhile, life goes on apace, in particular on the fore-court where wild birds share what food is going with the bantams, including the chicks, which are a shiny black and look wonderfully healthy.

The other day they were all there, pecking up some mixed corn, when the postman called, and as usual Holly our Rottweiler bitch was trying to fling herself through the window to get at him, aided and abetted by Teena the terrier.

Neither would attack him if they did get out. But he doesn't know this and would rather not meet them. So we always leave the outer front door ajar for him. He just slips the mail inside and closes the door before departing.

But for some reason the dogs were particularly exuber-ant. So much so that it looked as though they really could come crashing through the window to land in the middle of the crowd of birds below. And those birds were well aware of the danger. For they got smartly out of the way . . . all except the two defenceless little chicks.

I rushed back to the living-room to restrain the dogs and holding Holly, I looked out. Those chicks, quite unaware of any danger, were sparring with each other as if about to fight while their mothers, some yards away, had their heads together in one of those earnest talks that I do not understand.

Soon the postman departed in his little red van and peace returned to the forecourt. The chicks resumed their meal, their mums continued their discussion, the wild birds returned and all was well again.

October

Some time after we had turned the light out, my wife, who has ears like a lynx, gave me a push in the back and asked if I could hear anything. I said that I could not, but got up and went to the window.

I switched on our powerful torch and there, right in the brilliant circle of light on top of the forecourt stone wall were two animals the size of domestic cats busily turning over an oxhead we had brought home for the predatory birds and animals who come to what we call the Place of Skulls.

As it was raining heavily, we had left it on the wall for the night. And what I at first thought were two small cats were not cats at all but full-grown wild polecats turning this heavy oxhead over to get at a fresh side.

In the brief fraction of a second I flashed the light on them they looked up at me, petrified. But before switching off I just had time to see five little ones all around them on top of the wall.

It was perfectly safe to leave them there because all the beasts were in the first two looseboxes, each one with top and bottom door fast shut. This was because of the wolves which escaped recently.

Although they have now all been accounted for, at that time they represented a deadly menace to our stock. We have had the one alarm which turned out to be false but we have been locking up everything: horse, two donkeys and geese in one loosebox, bantams in the other.

We did not worry about the two big cats. Tiny Tim and Puss, as they are always on the watch for foxes and can shin up the nearest tree if necessary.

Next time I looked out of the bedroom window day was dawning. Those polecats, the parents and four half-grown young ones, were still busy eating away.

*   *   *

Until I was 13 I believed that badgers belonged to the bear family. But a visiting cousin who had emigrated to British Columbia in his teens told me that I was wrong; that the badger, like the wolverine of the Rockies and foothills, belongs to the same tribe as the tiny weasel.

The catamount is the hardiest of the lot and is known to the Indians of the Rockies as Qui-qui-hatch, the Invulnerable Beast. In my opinion the badger comes next.

Just after my twelfth birthday a badger killed 14 of our hens, taking only one away, and the following night my father and I lay out for him along with the gardener, who was armed with a two-prong pikel or hay-fork. My father had a double-barrelled 12-bore shotgun, while I proudly carried my birthday present, a ·22 single-shot rifle.

It was not until the third night that he came again. My father fired three shots and so did I, but that beast still managed to get half a mile before we killed him. He had been hit five times—three by my father and twice by me. And any one of those shots would have killed a fox outright.

That is the only badger I have ever helped to kill. Generally they don't go for barnyard poultry, but this one was very old and had only four teeth left.

Of all our native wild animals the badger is my favourite. His nocturnal rovings give him an air of mystery; normally he is very shy and I have found that the best time to see him is either just before dark, or just before dawn, when it is half-dark.

Since we started putting down two or three oxheads a week in the bottom paddock for predator birds and animals (we have declared this patch of land a nature preserve and allow no guns to be used on it) the badgers which feed there, like the foxes, often leave quite late.

They can be quite noisy creatures if not properly on guard.

On the last full moon, just before the equinoctial gales, I took a couple of fresh heads down just before dark, and sat on the south bank where I was more or less invisible. High clouds sweeping up from the south west at high speed occasionally obscured the moonlight, but at intervals I could easily see for a couple of hundred yards.

Then I heard the badgers coming up, cosily chatting away to one another as they do when they are not expecting danger. One was full-grown and there were two smaller ones and they made a beeline for the fresh heads.

Abruptly, the conversation stopped, giving way to the gnash of strong teeth on bone. After about five minutes the biggest one reared up, got its forepaws over to the other side of a head, then deftly turned it over to reveal a fresh side.

Suddenly, my wife opened the front door of our house about 50 yards away, spilling a brilliant beam of light across the forecourt and showing up the badgers too. They immediately crossed to the edge of the paddock to hide behind a bramble bush.

My wife called me in to supper and on reaching the house I switched off the light and stood watching from the door.

And within half a minute the three greedy beasts were at their dinner again.

*   *   *

Since pine martens made off with three young bantams the other week, our geese have stayed on continual and effective guard for intruders.

Among them this year is a single newcomer. Black and white like its father, this goose had, for a while, remained nameless simply because we were unable to determine its sex.

However, that was settled a few days ago when a dog which lives down the lane was incautious enough to saunter across the paddock.

The geese were on the forecourt, saw him and dashed

down to attack. Alas, the three big ones got held up by the pig-netting along the lower half of the garden fence and cursing, had to waste time going round. Not so the named-on-the-spot Boy David. Not yet half grown, he was able to scramble through the netting and carry on alone.

Running, flying and giving tongue—if that's the description for the appalling noise he was emitting—he gained rapidly on the dog which looked round in anguish but, unable to summon more speed, stumbled and went a purler.

This gave the Boy David his chance to rush in and deliver several pecks with a sharp beak on the unfortunate intruder's belly. And by this time the other three had caught up and surrounded the wretched animal.

My wife and I long ago learned that once geese get really cross you just have to leave things in the hands of whatever merciful spirit happens to be around. And evidently in this case there was one. Suddenly all four geese seemed to run out of puff. That was the dog's chance. He got to his feet and with all his remaining strength made the few remaining yards to the fence, crawled through a hole and made for a swampy piece of ground.

There he vanished into the undergrowth to recover in peace.

In single file the geese returned to the forecourt, the Boy David proudly leading the way. Then they all had a feed of corn, although the poor Boy hardly got his share because the others were all over him with endearments.

Even Albert was nearly as bad and my wife said: "Well, after all that, even if David and Albert fall out as ganders do, he'll never go into the pot."

*   *   *

The present crop of wild fruit and nuts beats everything we have seen for the past three years.

Within a few steps of the house we must have 15 or 20 pounds of hazelnuts, ripe for the picking if only we had the time.

Our elder bushes are groaning and drooping under the

weight of berries as ripe as the nuts and which will make wonderful wine.

As to blackberries, I've never seen so many; we must have picked at least 20 pounds, either for preserving in the deep freeze for winter or for jam-making with a leavening of apples. Even so, there were too many for us to use. So we have given a lot away.

The past few years of food shortages have decimated the grey squirrel population. So the present season of plenty is warmly welcomed by the few that remain.

The other day my wife and I took Teena and Holly out for what turned out to be a very brisk walk. As they hadn't been out for some days except for dull half-hour ambles along the lanes due to the torrential rain, the dogs were more than delighted.

At the halfway mark we sat on a dry rock in the sun while the dogs gambolled about sniffing this scent and that but never far away. Then my wife drew my attention to what was going on in a hedge on a bank about 100 yards away.

There were two grey squirrels, running along the bank until they suddenly disappeared down a hole. Half a minute later out they came, to run along the way they had come, soon vanishing over a ridge in the hill.

I took out my watch. Exactly three minutes later they reappeared, popped into the hole and back downhill to where there are plenty of hazel bushes. They made a trip every four or five minutes, busily building up their winter store.

Soon it was time for us to get back to the cottage for lunch but before turning back we went to see where the little creatures' nest was.

And there it was, an old rabbit hole, deserted by rabbits (we have no more burrowers up here, just brushwood bunnies).

We turned away with the two dogs to walk home, but what did we meet? Almost ran into, in fact? Those two squirrels, each with a sort of spray of nut-shells in one hand, coming home.

Our two dogs took off in pursuit but we didn't bother. For they never catch them.

Indeed, the squirrels vanished down their hole, leaving behind a few nuts. But before we got home they would have collected these and brought back a few more. At least they won't starve this winter, no matter how cruel the weather turns out to be.

*   *   *

When I was a child I was always more interested in toads than frogs, for the simple reason that if a frog objected to my interest it would, with three or four agile leaps, easily outpace me and disappear.

The ungainly toad on the other hand could never seem to manage a jump of more than about a foot. It is also a drier beast than a frog and therefore much more pleasant to handle—as long as one doesn't object to the pimples all over its small body.

Even though these were said to be capable of ejecting a poisonous fluid with a very obnoxious smell, as far as I remember I never noticed or, if I did, I failed to find it unpleasant.

In the last week we have had a day or two of pleasant sunshine and on one of those I was basking on a heathery slope near a little pool when I saw a small toad squatting comfortably on a sun-warmed rocky outcrop a foot or two away.

Our little terrier Teena, who was also sunning herself by my side, saw this toad and gave it a push with one paw, not in the least meaning to upset it but merely out of curiosity. It just edged to one side.

Thinking that for all its small size—somewhat less than that of a fully-grown frog—it could have been years old, I remembered the story told by an old Egyptologist who unearthed a toad from a tomb that had been sealed several thousand years before.

To his astonishment, although a bit dry, this little beast showed definite signs of life after lying for a time in the hot Egyptian sun, shot out its tongue and captured an unsuspecting fly.

After half an hour and several flies later, it hopped casually away into the desert. End of story.

Subsequently I was told that a small amphibian weighing a couple of ounces could not possibly survive for years sealed up in a tomb in a desert climate and I suppose that is true.

But I do not mind and have continued to believe that such a thing could happen, and actually did.

While thus cogitating, I watched Teena and the toad on the outcrop. Now that little thing knew perfectly well that we both knew it was there. Had it been in the least bit frightened it would have feigned death and remained on its rock without moving, for as long as we were there.

But without the slightest fear it stayed put, perfectly comfortable in the warm sun, not bothering even when Teena pushed gently with a paw to make it move. It moved, and that was that.

Only when she bent her head to sniff at it and stuck out her tongue to lick it did the toad make an ungainly little jump out of her reach. It obviously knew that it would taste nasty and didn't want to upset the ignorant little dog.

A little later a large buzzard swooped down to buzz us at very close range, passing swiftly overhead at a height of only a few feet. After it had gone, that toad was no longer to be seen. It had made itself scarce. And so we went home to lunch.

*   *   *

Although we've not had the snow that was threatened soon after that freak snowfall in Montana, north-west USA, it has got appreciably colder up here in the hills. The Montana fall was a month or six weeks earlier than usual and so was the temperature fall here.

Old Puss our so-called Persian cat, has slept on the next morning's kindling-sticks which line the floor of the open oven for a week now—at least a month before he normally does, which confirms winter will come early.

We have already had to start the bird-table going for the

smaller fry on the forecourt where, in the morning and evening, our bantams are fed the year round.

This year as early as mid-September between 15 and 20 chaffinches (mainly cock-birds) were joining in and by the end of that month they were accompanied by about half a dozen great tits and rather more tom-tits.

A few days later two robins and four dunnocks appeared, creeping about in their shy way. So food for them was sprinkled along the wide top of our dry-stone wall.

We no longer let the geese on to the forecourt as they are rather too aggressive with the smaller birds. They feed in their own paddock between the haybay (where they lay their eggs) and the duck-pond in the Old Garden.

A fortnight ago my wife returned from shopping with a most sensible titmouse nut-dispenser, cylindrical and all metal save for three wooden perches stuck through the mesh. We were going to put it up in the blackthorn tree in front of the living-room window when suddenly my wife pointed to the top of the window.

"That's an ideal place! We can watch them without getting out of our chairs—and it's only 12 feet away—if that!"

A hammer and nail was all I needed, and there it was two minutes later. We went inside and by the time we were comfortably seated with drinks in our hands, there were five tits, two great and three small, scrambling all over the nut-dispenser, upside down half the time and frantic with joy.

*   *   *

No doubt about it, there is already a distinct nip in the air both day and night.

And I have only to look out of the window to see that winter is just around the corner.

We seem to have a huge crop of sloes on the blackthorn bushes eight paces away from the front doors on the other side of the dry-stone wall, which happily gives access to those trees—and there is no need for a ladder.

Our only anxiety is that these berries are mostly only half

done, a few black, a lot brown and masses still quite green.

Let us hope there are sufficient to make three or four bottles of sloe vodka for winter.

Our winter woollies are hanging up on the living-room drying-line which—when it is not a wash-day—is normally stowed away out of sight. It is considered most unposh to have all the week's wash hanging in the living-room, but who cares? Certainly not we.

I was up quite early this morning. Well of course 7.30 is disgracefully late, even for someone like me. But it was quite dark when I heard shuffling sounds from the first loosebox, which is just the other side and adjoining my workroom.

I knew what that meant, and, if I hadn't, an outbreak of grunts and rumblings soon told me. The hedgehogs were back.

I warmed up a saucer of milk, broke up a piece of bread and put it out in front of the loosebox door, which was open.

Immediately Naomi, our jenny-ass, came forward to see what I had brought her.

But the milk was not for her. Pulling some ready sliced carrot from my pocket she was easily lured to the other side of the dividing wall, followed by her mum Rebecca.

I left them there, having closed the intervening gate. And to my astonishment, two hedgehogs were already at the saucer, slurping down the contents. Of me they took not the slightest notice other than to say thank you for the grub.

One of them was the colossal beast that Holly the Rott-weiler had already brought to the front doorstep after the dogs have had their midnight run round.

As soon as they had finished, they turned tail and waddled off for the rest of the day to sleep it off. But I think we have another two on the books until they go into hibernation. And they both look as fat as pigs. I think they will survive whatever horrors the winter may have in store for us all.

*   *   *

Weather-wise this has been one of the best months of the year so far.

We have had enough rain for the water people to breathe easily and it seems that in another fortnight our precious reservoirs will be filled sufficiently to keep us in water until next spring if the rainy spells continue.

But there is still no knowing what winter has in store for us, except that there are signs that it may yet be a hard one.

A few days ago my wife had put the goats out to graze in the north paddock.

And while she was tethering them she was also keeping an eye on the dogs, Holly and Teena. They are both very territorial and when running free never go outside the grounds. But in this case she was surprised to see Holly making friends with a young tabby cat we had seen around a few days previously.

It was a pretty little thing and we didn't know where it belonged. It was odd that Holly was making friends with it, because for a few days recently we had a friend and a young Rottweiler bitch called Molly staying with us.

Now, our Holly is always polite and forthcoming with dogs at shows, particularly with Rottweilers of her own kind. But here at home it was obvious that she was jealous of Molly. I suppose it is natural but it rather bothered us since my wife had been planning to buy a Rottweiler pup.

However, Holly certainly took to that little tabby cat. The other night she brought her into the house, obviously starving and with nowhere to go. Both our cats as well as the dogs accepted her. So we took her on.

She settled down beautifully and as she is very pretty and more than friendly, we are glad of her. She appears to be quite young now that she has filled out a bit, and shows no signs of having been neutered. There may yet be a few kittens on the farm.

*   *   *

Few of the predatory animals or birds eat shrew-mice because these little creatures have unpleasant-smelling glands which they put into action when attacked, making a horrible stink.

A cat will kill a shrew, of course, but will rarely attempt to eat it. Barn owls make a meal of them, though, swallowing them whole, and I believe badgers do, too.

I learned several hitherto unknown things about animals when I first read the Reverend Edward Topsell's book *Historie of all Foure-footed beastes*. For instance, to cure an "unhealing sore" on the foot—caused by a shrew running over it—all you have to do is catch a live shrew and put it into a small hole bored in an ash tree, and cork it up.

You then just take a twig from the tree and gently stroke the afflicted foot with it.

This book, I might add, was published in 1670, and I understand there are better remedies nowadays!

In another book, *The Arcadian Calendar*, written by E. D. Duming and charmingly illustrated by J. A. Shepherd in 1893, the foot cure is referred to and the author supposes that Topsell had in mind using only live shrews, bearing in mind the quantity of dead shrews one always finds lying about in the autumn.

But he gives no reason for this seasonal epidemic.

My own belief is that it has to do with the lack of insects—a staple part of the shrews' diet—when the weather turns colder, their numbers having already been depleted by the swallows and other summer visitors.

In captivity a shrew will eat four-and-a-half times its own weight in 36 hours. It manages this by eating for half an hour, then sleeping for an equal length of time, continuing this process day and night. If it cannot find this quantity of food, it quickly dies of starvation.

On a wonderfully sunny morning recently, I saw my first water-shrew for years. It was at the bottom of our pool, chasing the little water-boatmen which were frantically skimming the bottom in all directions, trying to escape.

The shrew certainly was having a fine time because the pool is always a hive of insect industry. So that is one shrew at least that won't die of starvation.

* * *

After several days of gales and heavy rain, with the barometer jumping about all over the place, the wind settled down to 3 to 4 on the Beaufort Scale, the temperature dropping with it.

The rain could turn to snow soon, though we fervently hope it won't because we've had quite enough foul weather so far this year.

Someone who lives nearby told us the other day that he had that morning seen a lone swallow still flying around near his place. Our swallows left long ago and this one must have been sick or too young to fly far when his companions left. Well, if this northerly wind lasts for 48 hours it will help him along famously. So I hope he has now made up his mind to depart. Otherwise he won't live long.

Other beasts react strongly to constant rain and storm-to-gale force winds.

The donkeys leave their loosebox for a swift bite either of fresh grass (of which there is plenty) or nettles that I have scythed down the previous day, but soon return to their quarters. Twenty-four hours of lying flat (even in constant rain with no sun) takes all the sting out of the nettles, enabling even Patchy the gelding to eat them, which he does with gusto, as soon as he sees Rebecca and Naomi attacking them.

Nettles, said to be very strong in protein, also make a very pleasant vegetable for us, provided they are cut when no more than four to six inches high.

Wild creatures are seldom seen in this kind of weather. Half a dozen ravens—locals living on or very near our land—can be seen pecking away at a skull in the lower paddock in the early hours of the morning. They are generally accompanied by a few carrion crows and maybe a little bunch of jackdaws, possibly a buzzard and (very occasionally) a kite.

The magpies seem to make the last hour of the day their feeding time when it rains, and they don't waste any of it either. And foxes, badgers, polecats and hedgehogs? I haven't seen one during the past three days.

As for our dogs: Holly and Teena, unlike the wild beasts

and birds, are always eager to be out and about whatever the weather.

In fact they become an utter nuisance, not to say danger. For every time anyone opens the door into the hallway they jump up, yelling madly, as if we are going for a walk. No dice, chums, look at that rain pouring down. Get some sleep in this nice warm room.

They obey for three or four minutes, then they are up again, trying to lick our hands or faces, even trying to sit on us to get us to stir. And I don't need to tell you that no dog weighing over a hundredweight can be tolerated for long as a lapdog. In fact, for my part, not for five seconds.

The other day, feeling that we needed exercise as well as the dogs, we decided to take them for a good long walk even though the rain was still pouring down.

We clad ourselves warmly while the dogs hindered us as well as they could by yelling their heads off and leaping all over the room. Finally we all got out, both dogs on leads, trotting jauntily along at my wife's heel.

When we turned them loose such was their joy that they raced about all over the place during the three miles to Gellygaer, which is our halfway mark. Although moving at full gallop, they never go further away from us than the permitted 100 yards at which point the whistle comes into use.

At the little pool at Gellygaer we were turning to go home when the dogs decided they wanted to have a splash in the water. Down they went and plunged in. Holly came out as my wife approached, jumped up, bowled her over, and next thing she was sliding down the mud on her behind, ending up waist deep in the pool.

She scrambled out, soaked of course, and she and the dogs did the whole trip home at a run, far too fast for me. By the time I got in, there they were, dogs stretched out around my wife who was sitting with her feet in a basinful of steaming water, and a hot glass of honey, lemon and rum going down nicely. I fixed one for myself and hoped that her unwanted dip would not result in a chill.

*   *   *

We have a very spectacular rowan tree about 30 yards from the cottage and since the last gale—which brought down a mass of the red berries—a pair of young magpies have set up house under its branches.

The smaller, probably female, bird has a damaged wing which is quite useless at present for flying. But she can, with her husband's help, get it nicely tucked up so that she can hop around to feed.

We have been putting some food down by the tree and as a result the pair have become quite tame in the five or six days they have been with us. So far, though, we have not been able to get near enough to pick the injured bird up to see what is wrong. Still, it doesn't appear to bother her much and if they have no further mishap it should be all right for them to fly away in another week or so.

Meanwhile, they are happily living under the rowan tree, quite unmolested by the other predator birds.

These include two buzzards which, up to the other morning, had settled down nicely with the magpies. I had put out a few bits of raw oxhead and a little corn, and when we came down to breakfast they were all eating contentedly, with the bantams doing likewise on the forecourt.

While we were watching, the two black bantam chicks, now about a month old, saw something going on down at the rowan tree and decided to get in on it. Off they trotted, closely followed by their mums.

On arrival they immediately tucked in, at first disregarded by the buzzards until one of them pinched a bit of meat from under the female buzzard's beak. She immediately squawked to her mate who obediently went for the chicks.

This was the cue for the two bantam mums to get into action. And though they are fat little blacks they are still enough of the gamecock to have neat little spurs, and the knowledge to use them.

As they raced to do battle they were joined by a cockerel which, although looking like a Rhode Island is still not too far from gamecock to know how to fight. The hen buzzard hid herself behind the treetrunk as her mate rushed to the rescue.

But the male buzzard was no match for the cockerel which took to wing and chased it halfway down the paddock before returning to his wives. The hen buzzard got back to the business of feeding, but it was a couple of hours before her mate returned looking quite ashamed of himself, poor thing.

*   *   *

Thank heavens we still have badgers up here. As far as I know there has been no official gassing of badger sets in the hills, for the reason that there is far less bovine tuberculosis in the higher altitudes where there is hardly any atmospheric pollution.

Badgers will eat practically anything and only in old age, when their teeth start bothering them, will they raid poultry. Wasp nests are their favourite dish, and this year, like previous years, we have only seen one or two wasps in the house, and one that got trapped in the car.

All sorts of other things are badger meat: slugs, snails, earthworms, voles, mice, young fledglings which have fallen out of their nests, even young rabbits. In the breeding season they often visit the roosts of our native pigeons and rookeries, in order to pick up any clumsy squab that has fallen from its high nest.

They will also eat certain roots and (occasionally) the bark of some trees. All in all, this wide diet keeps them fat most of the year round, and in rustic Ireland, I believe, badger hams are still a cottage delicacy.

The last full moon brought one of those clear nights, almost (as the saying goes, but it isn't true anyway) light enough to read a newspaper by. Dead calm it was, with the sky full of stars, plus that huge moon, and not a cloud anywhere.

It was curiously warm for the time of year, too, with the temperature still in the higher forties.

I thought I would go down to the paddock where every week we put down three or four oxheads, to see if there was any movement among the furry predators.

I was a bit early—it wasn't much after 9 p.m. when I got

to my vantage point, a bank where I could not be seen if I sat halfway down. There was no wind at all. So my scent would not be detected for more than a few feet in any direction.

I settled down to wait, comfortably warm and in no hurry. As it turned out, I was only just in time to see the first arrivals, a pair of foxes, evidently a vixen with the runt of her litter, a scrawny little thing all hide and bone.

They fell on a fresh head ravenously and as I watched I could see that the cub would need a lot more feeding yet before he would be in condition to face the rigours of winter.

After ten minutes there was a diversion. Three badgers, obviously one family, and all in good condition, arrived in a group.

Without any hesitation they went for the foxes, not angrily, but just, as one might say, elbowing them out. The foxes, after a few low snarls, gave in and trotted to another head, the vixen turning it over to get at the underside where there might be more meat.

The two groups went on feeding, sharing the same meal but ten or 12 yards apart, and apparently not taking any more notice of each other.

So it went on for about 20 minutes. I was getting chilly, the temperature having dropped several degrees since I began watching, and by the coldest hour of the night, an hour or two before sunrise, it would be freezing.

The badgers were the first to leave, though, ambling up towards the cottage, across the forecourt and into the top paddock.

The foxes went on feeding and didn't see or hear me as I got up to go, having seen enough to know that the oxheads are doing some good, and may even save the life of that painfully thin cub.

November

My wife had gone for her autumn visit to Manchester to visit her relations and to take up the Christmas presents.

This may seem a bit early for such goings-on, but early November is the last "safe" time of the year to travel far from the hills.

During her absence one thing happened that would not have been permitted had she been here.

Overnight I had left the week's oxheads (for the ravens and other predators) on the forecourt under the living-room window, instead of taking them to the Place of Skulls.

Next morning I opened my eyes to daylight, and there was an unaccustomed noise on the forecourt.

I got up and carefully approached the window, so as not to be seen by whatever happened to be making the noise. And well that I did.

All four cats were sitting straight up in a row on top of the dry-stone wall. But they—at least for the moment—were quiet and still. I didn't wonder either.

There, under my eyes, were the two oxheads glaring up at me from empty sockets. Surrounding them were four colossal ravens, each one busily breakfasting.

For about five minutes I watched them, fascinated.

All four were nearly the same size and one point was really remarkable. Carrion crows and rooks can sometimes only be described as tatty. Jackdaws and the rare chough are neat dressers. So are magpies and jays, which also belong to the *corvidae* or crow family.

But these ravens in their glossy coats with not a feather out of place, their black-gleaming and sharp-pointed beaks fiercely snapping off large pieces of raw meat, were really something to see.

Then Black Tom our senior tom-cat (incidentally the only polydactyl or many-fingered one of the four) looked up, saw me and let out a yell. Immediately the ravens spotted me and were off to the Place of Skulls to await their heads.

I am often asked if polydactyl pussies are common. And the answer is that they are not nearly so rare as some people think. I introduced them to this district nearly 20 years ago and, being wonderful hunters and therefore great travellers, they have spread far and wide at least in an eight-mile radius from our old farm on the other mountain.

While on the subject of cats, another reader recently wrote saying that as an animal-lover I should be ashamed of myself, turning poor little pussycats out at night, in lonesome country like this, and apparently in all weathers.

There's never any question of *turning*. It is always a matter of jumping up from a comfy chair and running to *let* them out.

The only one at all fussy in this matter is Cleo the Siamese, and as everyone knows they are highly-civilised pussies. Even Puss the black Persian, locally born and bred, thinks nothing of coming in after a rainy night out looking like a drowned rat to have a drop of warm milk and a nice clean-up in front of a hot fire, coming up all silky and glossy in half an hour or so.

* * *

A few days ago we were made aware that we have a small family of long-tailed mice or some such in the attic over our bedroom.

I had gone up to find out the cause of an occasional noise of something quite light-footed moving about in the faint light of dawn.

I poked my head up through the trap door on the landing ceiling.

And there, not six feet away, I saw two very small voles, each with a grain of corn between its fingers, having breakfast.

They were so small that they had not yet had time to learn what all wild things learn very early in life: to beware of anything bigger.

But these little things were not taken aback. They just gave me a glance and went on daintily enough with their meal.

And for perhaps the thousandth time I wondered at the incredible lightness of movement of these small creatures. They are, in my opinion, the easiest to tame of all wild animals. And what sweet and intelligent little pets they can become.

I was surprised to see them there because their nest was almost certainly not a foot away in a small cardboard box. This was lying on the floor against the wall exactly over whatever heat filtered through from the small paraffin stove in our bedroom.

There they would get plenty of warmth, no matter how cold it might get, while as far as food was concerned, the mother would be able to bring plenty from the granary without ever having to go outside, as all the thick stones walls of the house, from floor to the top, are honeycombed with old mouse-holes.

They had finished their corn and were carefully cleaning up their faces and whiskers with their paws, when my wife came upstairs accompanied by Holly the Rottweiler.

She went into the bedroom and Holly, evidently after a casual look around the room, gave a single questioning bark meaning "Where is he?" The little voles immediately sat straight up, listened for a moment, then, taking their time, hopped around the corner to their bed and vanished.

As to the mother, I never saw her but almost certainly she was somewhere in the walls, either on her way to or on the way back from the granary, with more corn.

*   *   *

There is always amazement in watching wild creatures performing feats without, as far as we know, having had any instruction.

Let's take, for example, the lowly snail. All it has for

protection is a flimsy shell which even the thrush—not a very brainy bird—can deal with.

Instead of wasting time pecking at the shell, the bird picks it up, flies to the correct height, then drops it on a flat stone. The shell smashes. One up to the thrush.

However, the snail knows a good trick, too. And when autumn comes he knows exactly what to do—which is why you see only slugs and never snails on a walk at this time of year.

I discovered the secret late in the afternoon one early autumn when I happened to see a snail coming out of a hole in a bank. Not realising snails were underground creatures, I sat down to watch.

The snail looked about, then moved off to a bit of weed which it cut and took back down the hole.

I marked the spot with a piece of wood.

Spring was well on before I saw that opening again, but the wait had been worth it. When I opened the nest I found the snail had carpeted the entire spherical interior with pieces of leaf and grass, sticking it all in one place with what I prefer to call glue, not slime. It was perfect, defensive and cosy too.

But some animals are not so lucky.

I have lived years in lands where skunks abound and where often, when travelling by train, one is hit by an appalling smell . . . a skunk on the line has heard the train coming and released its dreadful scent.

So it is with hedgehogs whose only defence is to roll up into a ball and extend their prickles—which is why they often pay the price—without even puncturing a tyre.

*   *   *

About a month ago one little bantam hen with one small cockerel chick hatched late in the summer took to frequenting my workroom by day.

I would be typing away under the window, or doing something on my knee-level workbench (which consists of one old railroad sleeper on four splayed legs), sitting on a three-legged milking-stood which is just the right height, when suddenly they would both fly down from the top shelf where all the Christmas decorations are kept.

One of the boxes there contains a dozen little silvered glass balls, and it is in this box that the hen, Mrs H, has taken to laying her daily egg.

But why, you may ask, is her half-grown son a necessary accomplice?

The answer is simple: in the first few days of this egg-laying, Mrs H appeared to have got a sore throat. In any case, instead of the triumphant "I've done it again!" cackle, all she could produce was a mournful croak. And this is where Sonnyboy came in, not with the opening bars of the "Londonderry Air" (thank God!) but with the usual hen-like announcement that another egg was there.

Even though, after more than a month, Mrs H is again in full voice at feeding time, Sonny feels obliged to keep helping out. And after she has laid her egg and he has inspected it to see that it is all right, she is perfectly happy to allow him to announce it to me.

I get up and open the door for them to go out and announce it to the rest of the world (Sonny obliging again), after which they both step down and join the assorted bantams plus the geese and any wild birds that may be in the vicinity.

At this point Mrs H (H is short for Hitler) takes over the task for which she was named: she proceeds to boss the lot, letting Albert the gander know with a sharp peck on the rump what she thinks of him if he allows his geese to presume too far.

She will also see a single magpie off, and heartily, too. But if five or six magpies arrive, you can bet it is the parents teaching three or four young ones the often far-from-gentle art of getting breakfast, dinner or supper. And of these she takes no notice, being herself too deeply occupied in selecting the finest grains of corn on the forecourt.

Sometimes we get several jackdaws from down-valley invading the table. We never mind because they are always very well-behaved, always keep in a bunch and take no more than their share. But Mrs H and Sonny are always at their most belligerent with them because they know that jackdaws are far too polite to answer back.

A few days ago, I had gone out to replenish the grain, and having scattered it went to sit on the mid-court wall between the stables and the cottage-front. Presently half a dozen jackdaws alighted—regular visitors who know my wife and myself to be quite harmless.

Suddenly there was a muted racket from my workroom window, and there stood Mrs H & Son, giving tongue (beak, rather) with furious wing-flaps and jumping up and down in frustration. But we waited until the jacks had finished before letting them out. And then what did they do?

Next best was the answer. They went for several cock chaffinches which were peacefully feeding. But much to the disgust of those two very cross bantams, the chaffs were much quicker, flew to the other end and went on feeding there.

*   *   *

The weather forecasters have been predicting snow in the north and when that happens we can get it down here too.

It didn't happen, but yesterday evening just as it was getting dark, our geese, which should have gone to bed, started kicking up a row.

This went on for quite a while until my wife put the dogs out. For a few minutes silence reigned but then it all started again.

At first we didn't think much of it, as the local hunt had been going through nearby coverts on our particular hill, and that might have kept foxes on the move.

They would have been too busy avoiding hounds during the day, and as the snow did not look likely, we felt that there could be a marauding fox or two sniffing around.

So, as the geese would not quieten down, we thought we would take a round with the dogs.

Later, on the way home with them, it occurred to my wife that she might see that all was well in the looseboxes. For the bantams occupy the floor-space of one while our four geese sometimes sleep in the other.

I stayed outside with the dogs while she went into the first one, now occupied by Patchy, her skewbald.

But having bestowed a pat on his rump, my wife went past Patchy to close the door of the downstairs little granary, and gave a gasp. For a large she-badger pushed past her and gave what I took for a friendly grunt as she went past me, across the muckheap and cut down the paddock as she ambled off homeward.

She gets about quite quietly and is well known to all our animals. Several times I have seen her coming up to the stables for a feed with her young when she has a new brood.

My wife followed her, telling me that the badger had finished off the small garbage-can of goat-feed, to which, of course, she was welcome, and that was that.

Shortly after we went to bed, and another night passed peacefully without snow.

*　　*　　*

Teena, the ex-hunt terrier, reminds me strongly of the first two dogs I ever owned, my twelfth birthday present from my parents.

They were Airedales, a dog and a bitch I named Tarum and Eatum. Not house-dogs because we already had a houseful, I made their bed in the saddle-room.

During the school holidays I was with them nearly all the time, sometimes even sleeping on a camp-bed in the saddle-room.

Teena reminds me of them so strongly that to me she's old times again. And she's a wonderfully good little watchdog, generally on the alert on the window sill before Holly the Rottweiler when there's a stranger about.

The other morning, having had their early walkabout, they were standing side by side and as good as gold, so as not to disturb the bantams which were busy on their mixed corn breakfast, when my wife said, "She's a rum-looking animal."

Teena slowly wagged her long tail, reminding me very strongly of Tarum and Eatum and those lovely days of my childhood.

"Holly?" I asked, just to be awkward.

"No!" she replied as Holly, hearing her name, threaded her way carefully through the chickens, followed by little Teena. They sat down in front of us with their *Aren't we good?* expressions, hoping for a biscuit apiece.

I went to the kitchen on my wife's orders to get a couple of those little fig-rolls of which we are all so fond. Presently both dogs had had their reward, but don't ask me what for, when suddenly Teena turned and put her nose up to Holly.

Politely, Holly put hers down to touch noses like the Eskimos' kiss when both dogs jumped violently apart, Holly emitting a short, sharp feminine shriek.

We were both helpless with laughter, and I remembered the days when I, too, used to generate far too much static electricity.

Once I was about to kiss a girl when, just as our lips touched, there was an explosive crack and that girl jumped backwards and planted a ringing slap on my inoffensive cheek.

But evidently Holly was more of a lady than that girl. For having carefully brushed her nose with the tip of her paw, she bent down again to see if there was any static left.

* * *

So far we have only had one November frost and that was not a hard one, for which small mercy we can thank inscrutable providence. Though who is to say that in a few days' time we may not be two feet deep in snow?

The wild birds are taking full advantage of the mild spell and making the most of what berries and nuts are left without bothering about the bird-table.

And Patchy, my wife's skewbald gelding, can still enjoy the freedom of the paddock.

His old water hole at the bottom of the farm is now an impenetrable bog and he doesn't often go there now.

Which is just as well. For it means he doesn't get his shoes sucked off in the mud as often as he used to.

Considering the way shoeing prices have risen in the last 15 years or so that is just as well. For in Patchy's young days a set of hand-made country blacksmith shoes cost £2 a set of four. Today a set made by the same farrier costs £9.50 up here. In other parts of Britain it can cost double that.

Patchy is always proud and pleased with himself when he gets a new set of shoes and the other day my wife was riding him back from the smithy when they got to that part of the village where there is the only shop with a big enough window for him to see a full reflection of himself.

When there was a blacksmith in Lampeter he used to love riding down the main street so that he could see himself in the big shop windows on both sides and it was laughable to watch him showing off to all and sundry. But the blacksmith there retired about ten years ago and we had to change, much to Patchy's sorrow until he found the big-windowed shop in the new village.

Well, there he was doing his Narcissus act with new shoes on when a car drew up and parked in front of the shop, blocking his view. The driver got out and was going into the pub opposite for a drink when Patchy turned crossly on the car and was just about to lash out a double kick at it when my wife stopped him.

The driver turned and asked her what was the matter. Almost helpless with laughter, she told him and so, very decently, he got back in the car and drove round the corner into the pub parking-ground.

Having watched the horse do his stuff and had a good laugh, he went in for his drink and my wife came on home without further incident.

* * *

We named our gosling David because he is exactly the same colour as Albert, his proud sire, and we therefore assumed that he was of the same sex.

But we still can't be sure, even though he is now nearly eight months old. He does show signs of being more his mum's little girl than his dad's big boy. So we may have been wrong in assuming him to be male. I hope we were. For father and son would be for ever fighting, and as the unlucky David had a very nasty accident a couple of months ago he'd be no match for his father.

The accident was caused by the terrific gales we had during the last week of September. We knew something was wrong when the geese didn't arrive for their morning feed and when we went down to the paddock the three adults rushed at us gobbling at the top of their voices to tell us what was wrong.

Then we saw, and started to run. For a cracked willow had fallen across poor little David, pinning him down.

It took only a moment for me to lift that small tree and for my wife to pick the gosling up. He made no resistance as she carried him to the house, hindered as we were by three huge geese all asking what was wrong.

At first we feared that his right leg might be broken but it was difficult to make a close examination without hurting him. So, as he seemed quite happy, we settled him down in a loosebox.

After lunch my wife went out to him, returning ten minutes later grinning from ear to ear, telling me it had only been a dislocation and she had slipped it back into position quite easily. So we both went out, and David awkwardly got up and hobbled towards us, gobbling out his thanks.

He was very lame, though little by little he got better until now it's hardly noticeable. But the other day there could have been a setback.

I was feeding the wild birds and bantams on our part of the forecourt. The geese were waiting for theirs on the stable side of the dividing gate, which is a two-bar affair with a line of logs underneath to stop them getting through.

Then Albert strode furiously forward, knocked one log down, stepped back about five yards, *and flew over* the whole gate.

David, evidently thinking that his dad had knocked down the log for him to fly through, did his best, and next moment became firmly jammed between the logs.

I pulled him out, tossed him over to his dad, and opened the top bar for the ladies. But I had seen that David made a perfect landing and wasn't limping any more. So all is well.

*   *   *

Hoping very much that I am wrong, I feel that an early winter looms.

A few days ago we had our first snowfall, and it lay on the ground for a good 36 hours in places where the sun couldn't get at it. Since then we have had a few milder days, but still with temperatures several degrees lower than usual for the time of year.

And another sign that severe weather is on the way: the marsh-tits have come up from their slushy but generally luscious-with-insects spot at the bottom end of our eastern boundary and are haunting the four blackthorn trees just to the far side of our stone wall.

At present they are quite happy with the split halves of the first fruit of the coconut season and, also hanging from those trees, a large lump of old-fashioned suet that they know how to shred for themselves. These birds are not alone, though. For every other variety of our local tits are with them, all busy putting on a bit of fat before it gets really cold.

I'm busy too, looking out various other small bird-table contrivances, including one of my own invention—a brilliant bit of brain-work that occurred to me a few winters ago when a lump of suet weighing at least half a pound was hijacked by a very large local buzzard.

This bird, although usually so beautifully mannered at the table that even the smallest of tits could easily drive him away, had seen this piece of suet and was determined to have it for himself. Waiting for just the right moment —when there were no tits about—he took hold of it with both claws and actually managed to tear it free.

He flew away with it but its weight pulled him to the ground in the first five yards. But on landing he jumped, still holding his prize, and managed, in five or six flying leaps, to get about 30 yards down the paddock, landing on a stone bank. Cleverly he rolled the suet down the other side out of sight of the bird-table area, and started to eat.

Within minutes there were five or six magpies in the trees around him but they, too, are well-mannered and waited for him to eat his fill. Presently he had had enough and flew heavily away, which gave the mags their chance.

But a huge lump of suet was too much to lose in this way. So I put my thinking cap on. And next morning came the result.

I put an eight-pound brick on the forecourt with four lumps of suet firmly tied to it with binder-twine. And nothing has ever tried to remove that.

For another bird-feeding contrivance I owe thanks to a reader. Two or three seasons ago I was sent a most useful device consisting of a ten-inch length of three-quarter-inch copper tubing closed at the bottom end and turned down at the top to make a hook to hang it up by. All down the sides were holes for the tits to get at shelled peanuts inside, and they simply loved it.

When we used to hang up the more common string bag of nuts, our chickens would fly up into the tree and rip it open.

For ourselves, with a population of at least 50 assorted tits, I have since made a much bigger nut holder, nearly three inches in diameter and holding a pound of nuts —which lasts three days in a bad winter.

That holder is now up joining the one my wife put up in October, and the other morning I went to the living-room window, having just come down to make the early tea, and what did I see?

There were two grey squirrels, one each side of the nut dispenser, putting their arms down the top and pinching the contents as fast as possible.

I had time to see that they were very thin but totally alive; and they are certainly welcome to anything on my bird-table that will help them survive the harsh winter ahead.

*   *   *

I happened to look out of the window just as something

flashed past on the forecourt, though not so fast that I couldn't see what it was.

And I was delighted. For I had glimpsed a pair of red squirrels. And these are very rare nowadays.

I hadn't seen such a beast anywhere on this smallholding or anywhere near it for most of this year.

There is a place several miles away where a pair used to live but we haven't seen them for months. I presumed that they had fallen victim to the mysterious disease that, I believe, is responsible for decimating the red squirrel population in recent years.

It used to be said that the grey squirrels were the culprits by driving the reds away from their favourite feeding grounds or by trying to exterminate them on sight.

It is generally accepted now, though, that the greys are innocent; that some unknown disease is to blame for the near total loss of our native breed and not the fell attentions of the American invaders, the grey squirrel.

Very cautiously and without making a sound so as not to disturb the dogs, I went out of the house to see if I could find out why those two little reds had come here. I was lucky, because there they were over the garage sitting in the top of our best hazel-nut tree.

When they saw me they immediately went on the offensive, sitting up, shaking their fists at me and cursing loudly.

They had already made good use of the tree because there at my feet were the emptied shells of four hazel nuts.

Pleased that they were making themselves at home, I retreated, hoping that they would stay, and went back to the cottage.

Several hours later I returned furtively to the scene of the action. But now there was nothing more to see except the husks of a dozen or so hazel nuts, all empty, and a scattering of shells. That showed me that those squirrels had enjoyed a good feed on the spot. I hoped they had also taken a few nuts away to make a winter hoard.

It does seem that they are here to stay. For now, five days after I first saw them, they are still around and don't take any notice of me or my wife if we come out of the house without the dogs.

*   *   *

My wife discovered the tragedy after going out at dusk to give the stock their last feed of the day.

The geese, Victoria and Albert, were not there. So, having fed the bantams, she went off in search of them. She was not long in the finding. Down in the paddock Victoria was lying dead with a broken neck, with Albert standing guard over the body.

Further down the paddock was the culprit, and my wife got a good view of him. He was a big animal, more brindle than red in the light of the dying day. It was definitely not one of our foxes, which arrived during the second winter that we were putting out between two and three oxheads a week for predators. I had thought that if we tried to feed not only the feathered robbers (which are plentiful) but could entice foxes, badgers, foul marten and so on, they might not take so many newborn lambs in the spring.

And so that turned out. Our foxes came regularly to feed once they realised that they were not being enticed to a hidden gun waiting to kill. They live in an old earth near the tree where our ravens nest in a repaired grey squirrel drey and have never taken any of our stock.

Soon the penny dropped. Neighbours of ours had been losing poultry regularly to a fox or foxes. So the husband bought a shotgun.

Shortly afterwards they had a good offer for their farm and sold it, buying a smaller one about a mile further on. They took all their stock with them and settled nicely in their new home.

Their old place lies only five minutes away from us across country, while their new one is a good long mile away. And now their fox, unable to account for the sudden loss of his food supply, had obviously discovered us and our stock.

We are conveniently near and he would never have heard a shot fired on our land as it is generally known around and about as a sanctuary for birds.

I decided to keep watch the following day in case the marauder returned to see what had happened to his goose. However, it was a foul afternoon, bitterly cold with an easterly drizzle, and I put off the vigil. But as my wife went out with the next evening feed there came the fearful racket from where Victoria had been killed.

Running to the corner of the forecourt she saw, about 40 yards away, the same fox now fighting off Albert who, with enormous wings beating and beak wide open emitting fearful language, was attacking him furiously.

My wife added her powerful and high pitched tones to Albert's and that was enough for the fox which vanished at full speed.

After herding Albert back to the forecourt we managed to get him penned in a loosebox with the help of the previously mentioned neighbours, who had come round for a drink.

Since then Albert has gone into the loosebox after his evening feed and waited for us to shut him in.

The bantams all roost safely out of that fox's reach, half of them in the loft granary where they all lay their eggs and the others—at least until the real cold arrives—in a tall elderberry bush.

But in any case the fox got such a shock on his last visit that I would be very surprised if he decided to risk paying us another call.

* * *

My wife had already gone to bed when I put the dogs out for their last run-around but Teena was back in one minute sharp to get centre place in front of the fire which was bright red down to the bottom bar, with a couple of logs banked with ashes so that it would still be bright and hot come morning.

This left Holly, for whom I gave a yell. Incredibly there was a muffled response as if she had a mouthful of feathers; but no Holly. Her answer had given me her position more or less. So I put the powerful torch on her, spotting the gleam of her eyes about 50 yards down the well paddock, slowly approaching.

Then I saw that she was carrying something quite big in her mouth and hoped that she hadn't repeated her trick of picking up enormous hedgehogs and bringing them up on to the forecourt. But now all the hedgehogs are, or should be, nicely tucked away in their winter hidey-holes and in the deep sleep.

Holly came nearer, got up on to the forecourt, and into the range of the hospitality light when I saw, to my amazement, a more than half-grown rabbit, hanging limp from her mouth as if dead.

I was also more than surprised to see that she was carrying it in the correct way like a gun dog, although she has had no instruction in gun ways.

But then, neither has she had very much instruction in the art of a sheep or cattle herder. And yet she had it instinctively from puppyhood.

Slowly, and very proudly, she brought it up and laid it down at my feet. Thinking it dead, I picked it up by its hind legs—but immediately it kicked violently and went on kicking.

I nearly dropped it but managed to get it into a more comfortable position when it calmed down. I took it up to my wife and we examined it carefully, to find it completely unhurt, save for a small patch of hair missing just between its ears.

Obviously it had been charged by one of the dogs, quite possibly Holly. They always do it but never catch them.

However, that night was very dark, with a northerly wind and snow in the air, several degrees of frost already turning the grass white. The rabbit had obviously run head on into a tree and momentarily knocked itself out.

The best thing would be to turn it loose near the well paddock gate where I had first seen it. So I took it back to that spot and set it free.

For a moment it sat still. Then giving the double alarm stamp with its powerful hind legs, away it ran towards where I knew there was a big bramble patch. So I lit it on its way and saw it vanish into its run.

Meanwhile my wife had been rewarding the dogs (reward one and you have to reward them both) with doggy chocs. And I poured us each a drink to toast them with. And then we went to bed.

December

Although that beautiful little bird the kingfisher generally nests in or under the banks of rivers and the larger tributaries, most of his hunting is usually done on little feeder streams, nicely stocked with water insects, small minnows, and baby troutlings that make for easy catching and easy eating.

But there generally comes a time when conditions change, as happened here last week. First we had torrential rains, and on one occasion saw a cow elbow-deep in her flooded field with a rabbit sitting on her back.

As we watched from the warmth of our car that cow ambled along towards the edge of the flooded area and by the time she was fetlock-deep in the water the rabbit walked along her back to the shoulder, when he jumped down to dry land, sprang a few feet through the air, and ran off. This is not an uncommon sight in such conditions. For although rabbits are strong swimmers, like anyone else they are not above taking a free lift to dry land. After the rains we had our first hard frosts. Our local river was too deep to freeze over but higher up the mountain at our level there wasn't a small stream running.

The other day, when it was bright and sunny, we stopped the car at one of our river's many bridges.

Suddenly, about 50 yards up river we saw the unmistakable flash of a kingfisher as he flew fast towards us, to alight in a tree 20 yards away.

"He just seems to be resting," my wife said . . . and a penny dropped. When the smaller streams freeze up those little fish that can get away go to deeper water that won't be so likely to freeze. And, of course, the kingfishers go with them.

We watched this particular bird for a good five minutes before it took to wing and passed by, flying fast not six feet above us. Kingfishers are solitary birds and do not gather in flocks.

We decided to drive to the next bridge, a couple of miles lower down, and when we got there, stopped in the middle.

We were looking in opposite directions when something quite remarkable happened. Fifty yards farther down river I saw a similar bird take wing and at that very moment my wife caught sight of the first one coming towards us, flying high above the middle of the river.

Again it came to rest 20 yards away and four or five minutes later it flew as before, straight over the car and away down river.

We were fortunate to have witnessed a move by the birds to the milder weather of the coast, something I had read about but neither of us had seen before. So we went happily on our way, wishing both those little fishers their equivalent of *tight lines*, otherwise *a sharp beak and happy diving*.

*   *   *

With a ton of soft coal and four tons of freshly-cut beech logs we should be all right for the winter, however long and severe it turns out to be.

Heating the house is an easy operation; there are many others, such as laying in supplies of fodder for the stock, including our bantams. These are producing such a surplus of eggs that my wife says we will have to eat an omelette every other day for the next week. Which proves the biddies are getting the right quantity of the right kind of food.

Since last Easter, we have been feeding them on the forecourt, without thinking that this forecourt is also where we feed hungry birds in the winter time, and the cockerel might resent them.

Strange to say, he did not. The only one who did a bit of

chasing was the little round black called Martha. She didn't
see the need for a mass of small wild birds gobbling away as
though against the clock. But then it was pointed out to her
(I think by Cocky our gentleman-bantam) that it was a
waste of her own valuable eating time to chase silly little
birds that took no notice except to jump about six inches out
of her way, causing her to skid wildly on her turns. She saw
Cocky's point and thereafter gave up the chase.

Great tits, tomtits and of course the marsh-tits are always
the first to ask for coconut on the half-shell, nicely suspended on a bit of baling twine, not to mention peanuts
likewise suspended from the blackthorns.

Mrs Hitler, the pullet who sat on Martha's eggs when she
abandoned them, and hatched them out, proudly raising
them, had noticed the antics of the tits on the coconut
half-shells and the peanut bags and thought she would
have a bash.

First she flew at a coconut, only to find herself on a
wildly-revolving swing which spun her into a blackthorn
twig all covered with nasty black thorns, one or more of
which may have pricked her. With an indignant squawk
she fluttered down, but she was not yet defeated. For my
wife had just finished (with the help of a kitchen chair)
tying a peanut bag on a sycamore branch somewhat higher
than the blackthorn.

Mrs Hitler watched. And when my wife had finished the
job and returned the chair to the kitchen, came back to
watch with me from the living-room window. Mrs Hitler
couldn't see us and so, all being clear, she flew neatly up
but with a little too much power. She clawed at the branch
but it swung away from her, leaving her upside down,
which, as everyone knows, is the correct position for a tit,
with its beak within easy striking-range of the nuts. With
remarkable aplomb she took her stab but once again there
was too much power behind her beak. This time she let go
but, unable to turn fast enough, landed on the forecourt flat
on her back with wings akimbo.

Since then there have been no more assaults on the
nut-bags.

*　　*　　*

My wife had taken the dogs out for an early morning walk and as the weather was fine after days of rain, I had not expected them to return for two hours at least.

But they came much sooner than that because my wife had a tale to tell, and proof that it was the truth.

They had been fossicking about inside a big, derelict old farm building which had long been ownerless near the mountain top. If there had ever been protective trees there, they had all long been cut down; not one remained and there was no shelter in any of the buildings. For every useable slate had been removed to cover other buildings lower down the mountain.

Suddenly Holly the Rottweiler brought a soaking wet offering that she had discovered. It was a long-eared bat, still warm but unlikely to survive long if left.

My wife gave Holly a piece of dried liver as a reward for her intelligence and pocketed the little animal to bring home. Evidently it had found the weather too cold and its early-morning flight in an attempt to catch a meagre breakfast had been too much. So it had sought refuge in that inhospitable spot. If she could get it home and revive it, it might take up with our little group of pipistrelle bats and survive the winter.

By that I don't mean to say that it would actually join up with them because these small bats with their colossal ears, each nearly as long as the two-inch body, are rather solitary.

The species is found all over the country in small numbers except in north Scotland where they are not known. When hunting insects it will hover over a tree like a hawk. Then having chosen its victim it will swoop and pounce, often eating it on the ground.

Both dogs got another bit of dried liver on arriving home where the bat soon became quite lively. We hung it up on our indoor clothes-line where it seemed quite happy.

But after lunch we took it along to the top granary where the pipistrelles live in daytime and all the time if winter gets very severe, which I very much hope won't be the case.

It was a friendly little thing and never tried to bite us once. So we are both devoutly hoping that it will survive and live at least another year. Meanwhile today is Saturday and there it is up in the granary, hanging upside down on its nail in a beam.

* * *

As I write, it looks like snowing. And as my subject is a brilliant white cat, we may as well call him Snowy.

He has to be renamed because his last owner got his sex wrong, even persisting in her delusion after taking the cat to the vet to be neutered.

Then she decided to move to the North and asked us if we could take two of her cats. Both were shes, she said, and good in the house. So we said Yes, why not?

That was a week ago. The first thing we noticed was that Ermintrude was no lady, but Almost a Gentleman. In other words, a neutered tom. He was in superb condition, and a perfectly sweet cat to boot, forever on the purr and before he'd been here half a day my snuff-coloured trousers were all white below knee-level due to the hairs he had rubbed off on me.

He was also a skilled bird-killer, which seemed odd in view of his blinding white colour. But there he was catching a chaffinch in broad daylight—and that bird could have spotted him on top of the next mountain if he'd had his wits about him.

He didn't play with the bird, but killed it immediately and ate it feathers and all. This meant of course that he is a pro, which accounts for his amazingly good condition. But as this is a bird sanctuary something had to be done about it.

So now we are making sure that he does not get out in daylight.

He seems quite happy with this routine, spending most of his day fast asleep on his blanket in the kitchen, except when I go in there. The moment he hears my footsteps he is wide awake rubbing hairs off on my trousers, telling me he is starving on account of this bird-sanctuary business.

So I have to go into the larder, punch a couple of holes in an evaporated milk-can and give him a saucerful. He likes it thick and by God he gets it, because I always think *that saves another bird's life*.

The first time Teena the terrier saw him in her kitchen she attacked. But Snowy administered one short, sharp oath and smacked her across the snout with no more than one sharp claw out, quite sufficient to ensure there'll be no more trouble in that department.

So the birds are all right, as are the dogs and the cats. And as to what happens during the nights to the mice and rats—that is nobody's business but Snowy's.

*   *   *

We knew that winter was really on us as soon as we saw the marsh-tits near the bird-table. All this year we have kept it going with only this species absent from among the birds using it.

Evidently these brave and independent little things had found enough to live on in their marsh, a few yards from our eastern boundary.

But there they were on the blackthorn tree. Within minutes my wife brought 1 lb of suet to hang from the tree but before she had tied it up they were all around her, going for it.

Yet there had been nothing in the weather forecasts to indicate any change from the constant rain we had been suffering recently. But the night before the marsh-tits appeared everything changed. The glass dropped half an inch in 12 hours, the morning temperature was minus 5C (or 23F if you prefer it), and there was a sprinkling of snow on the forecourt.

I was down very early to put down two measures of food on the bird-table. It was crowded and for good luck I put a couple of handfuls on the living-room window sill. Before I had gone there were five marsh-tits on the bird-table, with three tomtits and one great tit on the nearest branch of our old moss rose bush.

Two cats were on the inside of the window, softly growling and slowly waving their tails. A marsh-tit bravely approached and pecked at the window. The cats yowled and wildly waved their tails.

"It's quite all right, chums," the tit seemed to be saying. "The boss is magic. He's put a force field round us. Those bloody cats can't get through. It's quite safe, see?"

He gave the windowpane a stiff and very audible peck and immediately attacked the grub. The cats' tails waved wildly and the owners growled horribly. But next second there were eight tits on the sill, just as wildly attacking their grub.

A minute or two later two dunnocks, one starling and two rather embarrassed-looking blackbirds were also making a good meal. One thing was noticeable—they were liberal feeders. In other words, they were not as finicky as I was as a child when, faced with a jamroll, for example, I always ate the jam first and reluctantly forced down the suety part afterwards.

Now, several days later, we know just exactly where we are: on the verge of a nasty winter and we thank God for the warning we had from the marsh-tits.

Thanks to them we knew what to expect and got ready for it. The other day we had run out of bird food and decided to go to town in the Land-Rover to stock up. We had some difficulty starting her because we had also run out of the usual "quick-start" push-button stuff. But I knew that anti-freeze mixture is also a good "quick-start" solution. So I squirted a little into our dear old Land-Rover's air intake and off she went, almost before I touched the button.

Today we are isolated and out of touch, with icy roads, and dire warnings on radio and TV. But we're all right. We have pounds of suet, pounds of coconuts plus enough for the other bipeds and quadrupeds on the farm to last for a fortnight. And we may need more than that.

*   *   *

Not so many years ago summer picnics could be a nightmare to people who feared wasps. Yet nowadays, even in the hills where lethal crop-dressings are not used, there is a scarcity of them.

In the last three summers two or three have hit the Land-Rover windscreen, I have seen perhaps the same number in the house, one or two flying about outside—and that is all.

This change in the ecology seems to be part of a chain reaction. Not so many years ago autumn was the fattening season for badgers. If you were up late enough, a little after sunset or half an hour before sunrise (generally the best time of the whole day), you could see them going about their business digging for various kinds of edible roots, a great variety of creepy-crawlies, slugs and snails, leather-jackets—all enemies of the farmer and gardener. As autumn slowly turned so these beasts grew visibly fatter for the coming winter.

Never all that fast on their feet, they seemed to get slower and slower if they had to run. And as they grew fatter, that run developed the roll of a drunken sailor, their hide wobbling from side to side as the layer of fat beneath increased.

Much of this fat was produced by wasps and their grubs. I've often watched them attacking wasps' nests, either in thick hedges or underground. They seem quite impervious to the stings.

Sometimes I wake early and if it is around six I get up, knowing that sleep is gone. And since the beginning of November, when we had our first cold snap, I have done a bit of badger-watching. It started quite by accident. I had made a mug of coffee and was brisking up the fire (never allowed to go out in winter) when I heard quite a loud noise outside in the Place of Skulls, where we feed the predator birds on oxheads.

It was pitch dark. So I went to the side door opening into the garage because it opens silently and I could hide behind the pick-up. The noise continued. I hadn't taken the torch out because I didn't want to frighten whatever it was.

I waited for about five minutes to get my night eyes. There was a half moon in a star-spattered sky and not a breath of wind. It was bitterly cold, with a very hard white frost almost like a thin fall of snow which, with that bright half moon, greatly aided visibility. And presently I could see clearly that what I had thought might be a fox, turned out to be two badgers, having a nourishing go at the freshest oxhead which my wife had put out the previous night.

These were full-sized beasts and should have been rolling fat. But they were not.

Already a faint line of light was burgeoning over the mountain to the south-east. Suddenly I shivered—and sneezed. For I had come out with no coat on. Those badgers jumped—and next moment were galloping away.

Well, they have been here several times since then which, according to those who say that badgers go into the deep coma of total hibernation, is wrong. Now I am going to see if our family butcher can provide us with a weekly bit of fat. I expect he will because he is a nature lover and very interested in anything that is wild and in need of a little winter comfort.

*   *   *

We never have to bother much about our goats. They have been trained to a fixed formula ever since we got them.

If it's a fine day, they are tethered to a breeze block in the north paddock. If the weather is foul, they stay in their own loosebox.

On this particular day—the last market day before Christmas—my wife had got a lift into town leaving me in sole charge of the property.

As the rain had stopped I let the goats out on to the forecourt so that they could pick about and get what exercise they could without doing any damage.

Then the time came for me to drive into town to bring back my wife with her shopping. But when I stopped in the drive to close the gate, I found Alice, our beautiful Nubian goat, standing beside me.

My neighbour, too, was there, driving his flock quietly along to change pasture with the help of a good dog.

He warned me that about 100 yards on my way I'd come across a lame ewe he had had to leave behind. He said not to pick her up as his son had already gone off to fetch a

Land-Rover in order to collect her and any other sheep that might have fallen out.

I was waiting in the lane for him to move on before getting in to start my engine—I did not wish to frighten the tail end of his flock—when I saw the lame ewe gallantly hobbling along the lane towards us.

When she recognised me with Alice she came up to meet us, Alice politely greeting her.

As Alice looked ready to stay there and look after her, I left them. Alice's first owner had trained her as a bell-wether, so I knew both goat and ewe would both be there in the drive when I returned.

I told them to stay as a shepherd tells his dog and drove off. Sure enough, when I returned a full hour later, they were both there.

Within a few minutes my neighbour's son arrived and we got the ewe into the back of his Land-Rover without any difficulty.

This was the end of the story as far as Alice was concerned . . . except to say she was given an extra ration of her favourite sugarbeet for being a good girl and a good bell-wether.

* * *

Last summer, when two red kites were nesting just a few miles away, we sometimes used to walk the dogs in that direction just to see how the pair was getting one.

Then they disappeared. I don't know exactly why— probably some fool egg-collector had been messing about there.

In my boyhood many kids collected eggs, some of them even ending up with collections worth many hundreds of pounds. Today the hobby is illegal, and rightly so because within the last 40 years or so disaster after disaster has hit our native feathered creatures of the wilds.

Today, a small group of enthusiasts are trying their hardest to increase the population of the kites in Southern and West Wales. But they are not having all the success they deserve—thanks almost entirely to egg-collectors.

A few days ago I learned something about kites which corrected a false impression I have had for years about their lack of bravery and skill.

Kites only occasionally appear in this column because they are a rarity on the bottom paddock, which is where we put oxheads for predatory birds and beasts. Regular visitors do include eight ravens, many carrion crows, occasional rooks, jackdaws, magpies and (I'm glad to say) two jays.

Then, a few days ago, a beautiful pair of kites appeared in the paddock. As there were already two pairs of ravens plus an assorted medley of carrion crows, magpies and two buzzards there, we expected to see these kites sent packing. And as we expected, the attack on them was made.

The two fork-tailed kites shot up into the air emitting harsh noises as they went. Then, without even bothering to hover awhile as hawks do, each one shot down like fighter planes on to the two largest ravens, our original pair who nest in an old squirrel-drey.

Those ravens immediately flew away, heading for home, but they were no match for the kites' speed and acceleration, as testified by the black feathers that came floating softly down to earth. The kites, in turn, were being followed by two pairs of younger ravens but these could not catch up, although they were trying hard.

At the same time the two buzzards quietly leaked out of the landscape, by the back door as you might say, but fast. And as the older ravens vanished into their beech-tree drey, the kites, still at full speed, turned as on a sixpence to scatter the young ones, who immediately turned and vanished over the nearest hilltop.

One might have thought that between 15 and 20 mixed magpies and jackdaws would then have closed ranks. But they, too, dispersed as the kites flew back.

For the next 20 minutes the kites thoroughly enjoyed the prize of victory—the freshest oxhead in the paddock. Then they flew away and the other birds returned. Everyone was happy.

*   *   *

The other day we were out in the car far from our usual
haunts after a visit to an old friend when we got into one of
those unfortunate fog patches common in the countryside
at this time of year.

We were on a three-lane road with visibility not more
than 50 yards, though the fast and middle lanes were full of
cars and those terrifying articulated lorries averaging about
50 mph, some with only their side-lights on. We stuck to
the slow lane doing about 20 and glad to let anything pass
us that wanted to.

It was the safest place to be and we were quite happy
there, not anticipating anything nasty, when suddenly,
right ahead and on the very edge of the road was a fairly big
dog sitting with one front paw held up in front of him.

With a quick glance rearward I pulled over and stopped
and we both jumped out. We soon had that dog in the car,
on my wife's lap because we had Holly the Rottweiler in the
back and she is not at her best with large strange dogs
except at shows when she is always ready to make up to
anything from a Saint Bernard to a two-pound Yorky.

Meanwhile the stranger was pathetically grateful, particularly after a couple of Polo mints, which also served to
make Holly feel better about the intrusion. She was a
beautiful young retriever bitch with what appeared to be a
badly-sprained shoulder which would be easy to treat,
provided we could first get a clue as to her owners.

That was soon forthcoming because we came to a police
car by a café in a layby. The two policemen in the car
immediately recognised the dog, knew the owners and said
they would telephone them from the café and take her
home. As we were in a hurry to get home we left her with
them and carried on after taking a note of the owners'
number.

As soon as we got home we phoned them and found that
the vet had already seen the patient and that she would
soon be all right again.

Evidently that dog, which already knew how to undo
and shut a house-door, had learned how to undo a car's
also. From now on they would lock both back doors of the
car whenever she was in the back seat alone.

*   *   *

As we finished off our Christmas shopping, I stopped the Land-Rover and looked towards the hills, behind which our cottage nestles.

In town it had been raining ever since we arrived, but on leaving home earlier sleet had been falling on top of a hard night frost. Now, to my horror, I saw that there was an even coating of snow from the hilltops down to about 800 ft above sea level.

Obviously we had to hurry back before conditions got worse.

Once we reached the snow we had to use four-wheel crawler drive, which one doesn't use unless absolutely necessary because petrol consumption rises to almost twice normal.

Then came the welcome sight of our chimney, smoking away to show that the wind was coming from the north. The snow was so thick that visibility was down to 20 yards. It was uncannily quiet. The forecourt was empty. There were no birds in the blackthorn trees, not a tit on any of the three hanging coconut shells.

While I was putting the Land-Rover away my wife opened the front door and the four dogs poured out, returning to the warmth of the living-room as soon as they saw we were both home.

My wife then went to the nearest loosebox and, with one finger to lip, signalled me to approach.

Quietly I did so. And the mystery of the quiet forecourt was solved. There in the loosebox was huddled the entire stock of the farm. One large horse with a robin on his rump, the two donkeys Naomi and Rebecca, who had a robin warming itself on her shoulders, the bantams cosily cuddled up in a corner, plus various chaffinches, three dunnocks and two blackbirds, all hunting for hay seeds under the long rack.

My wife put out three feeds for the four-legged friends while I swept a clean patch on the forecourt. By this time the light was beginning to fail. But as soon as that patch had a measure of corn on it out came all the birds except the two robins.

Now robins are short-tempered little creatures and these

two have nothing to do with each other as a rule. One normally lives around the front of the house and the other at the back.

Generally when they are feeding in the cold weather one of them eats on the forecourt and the other behind my wife's dry-stone wall.

But when my wife went into the loosebox to shoo them out, they refused to leave. There they sat on Patchy's manger, one on each side. When she walked right up to them the only notice the nearest one took was to hop across to the other side of the manger. So there they were, side by side, making menacing noises and gestures.

However, Patchy, being a peacemaker by nature and very gentle, couldn't stand this. He gave the new arrival a push with his nose, and looked at my wife as though asking her to retire. She took a step back. The robin which had been pushed took the hint, and there it was, back again on its own side.

All three resumed their meal. Again peace reigned in the loosebox . . . and there was good will towards all.

*   *   *

As the big freeze-up continues, my wife and I are feeling well and truly cut off from the world.

We can't even start the Land-Rover. The battery is flat and Naomi the donkey has destroyed our old-fashioned paraffin engine-warmer. This usually burns day and night, keeping the sulky engine warm enough to be started by hand.

I was refilling it when the telephone went while my wife was in the haybay. So I left the warmer beside the car and went back to the house. When I returned (I wasn't long, it was just a wrong number) the two donkeys were in the garage and Naomi had one foot on top of the warmer which, alas, was squashed as flat as a pancake.

We put the battery on the charger in my workroom. And before bed time, as usual when re-charging, we disconnected everything.

And a good thing too. For next morning when I went to

reconnect, I found water dripping on to the charger from the ceiling. The hot water tank had sprung a leak in the night. So the charger is out of action for a day or two until dry.

Albert the gander was the victim of the next mishap. Since Victoria was killed by a fox he has taken up his quarters in one of the looseboxes with the bantams, the donkeys and Patchy, my wife's skewbald gelding.

Albert hobbled out on Christmas Day with a bruised foot, obviously the victim of a misplaced hoof.

It was while I was making sure that his injury was not serious that I was reminded what an enormous amount of heat a few birds and animals can generate.

During the night the temperature had dropped to minus 12 degrees centigrade, the lowest so far this winter, and there was about eight inches of snow on the cottage roof.

But to my amazement the two water butts fed from the roof over the granary were overflowing and full of ice. And on that roof was a bare, perfectly square patch immediately above the looseboxes. And even over the rest of the roof the snow was melting fast.

We haven't had water in the taps since the freeze started. But now, although we are still using snow water, all the donkey work has been done by our animals in filling up those butts.

Albert's foot already seems much better. Horses (and donkeys) hate treading on anything alive, as anyone watching the jump jockeys over the sticks at the National will know. And I can bet you that whichever beast was responsible whipped that hoof away before applying its full weight. And Albert bears no malice.

It only remains for me to hope that the New Year will be kind to us all—city, town and country dwellers alike.

*   *   *

Out for an early morning walk, we were about one-and-a-half miles from home when we heard the unmistakable sounds of Prudy, the fat, all-white cat we at first called Snowy, in a bad temper.

The noise came from a thick bramble patch and Teena the terrier was immediately on the spot. We were close behind, eager to find out what was making Prudy so angry all this way from home, from which he must have strayed much earlier, on what was one of the very coldest nights of the year.

Anyway, there he was, in a very uncomfortable fix. For he was completely stuck among the prickles and even with Teena doing her best to free him—an excited effort that seemed more likely to terrify him into an early grave than to secure his release.

After my wife pulled Teena away I bent down to free Prudy and it was then that I noticed a baby rabbit lying as if dead almost underneath the cat. Obviously Prudy had been chasing it when he became stuck.

I slipped the bunny into my coat pocket before getting Prudy out of his fix and lifting him to one side, whereupon he immediately sat down and proceeded to lick himself down. Then, as the sun broke out and shone brightly upon us, he rubbed himself against our legs, purring loudly. Which seemed unbelievable considering he had probably been trapped there in the bitter cold for hours.

By the time we turned to go home, I felt Prudy's little captive stirring in my pocket and soon it, too, had entirely recovered, having suffered no apparent damage other than a loss of consciousness.

When I put the little bunny down Prudy took no notice of it, never even sniffed at it. As far as he was concerned rabbit-chasing was better forgotten because it had got him into a very awkward position from which, had we not opportunely arrived to rescue him, he would have eventually emerged minus at least half his coat.

As Prudy sat there and watched, I put that young bunny down, gave him a little pat on the rump and let him go.

Teena jumped at him and let off a little bark under his tail, and away at a short gallop he went straight across the field to where there was another bramble outcrop, and into this he disappeared, to carry on into what, so far, had been, at least, an interesting New Year.